The Center
of the Universe

*Where Your Story
and My Story Meet*

Rita Kay Reese

ISBN 978-1-63903-462-8 (paperback)
ISBN 978-1-63903-463-5 (digital)

Christian Faith Publishing, Inc.
832 Park Avenue
Meadville, PA 16335
www.christianfaithpublishing.com

Printed in the United States of America

Before We Begin

I have a great idea for a book. My story would take place in Walmart. One day, some cataclysmic event would suddenly happen, and everyone who was in Walmart would be trapped there for days. My story would include interesting and strange well-developed characters, complex conflicts, romance and, maybe, even a murder. Best of all, it would be a dark comedy.

My dear friend, Alora, is considering writing her own book so she could help me write this amazing dark comedy. She is only fifteen but already a gifted writer. She could help make this story worth reading!

However, in light of all that we have been through as a nation, I am not so sure that you would want to read a "shelter in place" story. I bet you could write your own shelter in place story—a horror story for sure. Ha-ha-ha.

Alora's mom, Amy, suggested that instead of a dark comedy, maybe I should write my story—my life story. She suggested that I could share the healing grace, truth, and love of Jesus through my personal stories.

I am excited to share with you vignettes from my life. You will read snapshots of past experiences and events that have impacted me. These short stories are told in the voice of the child, teenager, or adult experiencing the story.

Storytelling and listening to stories is so much fun. Who doesn't love a good story, especially a story of victory, love, and hope! So what do you think? Is this a better idea for a book?

As you read my stories, it just could be that my stories will remind you of your stories. I know that you, too, have stories to tell. Your story is important and needs to be shared with others who know and love you. Sharing our stories with each other can be a healing experience. We can know each other, pray for each other, and love each other through our shared stories.

At that place of shared heartbreak, pain, or disappointment is where we will meet Jesus together. Jesus truly has been with us and continues to move in our hearts through our stories. It is through Jesus that we find true healing, hope, and love.

After each vignette, I will write a letter to you. I love writing personal letters. I am not talking about texts, emails, or instant messages, but good ole fashioned pen-and-notebook-paper words from the heart letters!

I started writing letters to encourage my friend Amy. Amy is awesome, amazing, and wonderful. Amy is a confident leader who has a passion for sharing the love of Jesus with others. She is a woman of many accomplishments. However, since she is a normal person, she has moments of insecurity and self-doubt. I don't believe that she always sees the beautiful Christlike woman that I see in her.

When you are a leader and a "public figure," you can become vulnerable to receive many texts, emails, and phone calls with words of encouragement as well as words and words and words of criticism. I can just imagine someone calling her to say, "God told me to tell you blah, blah, blah." Maybe he did. I don't know.

What I do know is that I wanted to be the voice of love and encouragement for Amy. I wanted to tell her every single day that God created in her a beautiful woman filled with love, patience, and compassion for others. I also wanted to tell her every day that I love her. Every day seemed a bit much, so I decided that maybe a once-a-week letter would be better.

So every Sunday, I would hand Amy a handwritten letter in an envelope with her name on it. She would simply smile and say, "Thank you."

While writing letters of encouragement over the years, God has given me a deeper understanding of true encouragement. I have learned that words spoken or written to encourage should not be *shallow* words of flattery. I tend to overuse *awesome* and *amazing*. Ha-ha-ha. Also, when we encourage, we need to be careful not to overuse phrases. When said too often, they become simply Christian platitudes. Example: "God's got this" or "God is in control." Those words, when said too often, can lose their meaning. They can become *hollow* words spoken.

Sometimes encouraging words should take the form of truth spoken from the heart. It is so much easier for me to tell someone that they are awesome and wonderful than to speak words of admonishment, truth, and light. Paul tells us in Colossians 3:16, "Let the word of Christ dwell in you richly, teaching and admonishing one another in all wisdom, singing psalms and hymns and spiritual songs, with thankfulness in your hearts to God."

I look forward to writing letters to you, my friend, to encourage you and remind you that God created in you a beautiful woman. I want to be the voice of love and encouragement to you through my letters. He has been at work during your life journey, and he is at work right now, today, making something new and beautiful in you. As you read, I pray that Jesus will reveal to you your true beauty in him.

So grab a cup of coffee or your favorite tea. Find that perfect, comfortable reading spot and come with me on a journey through my stories.

It won't be a dark comedy, but we are sure to find dark times as well as funny times in my stories. On this journey, as you recall your own story, I pray that we will see Jesus in our stories.

Remember, each story will be told to you from the viewpoint of the child, teen, young adult, adult, or "old lady," experiencing the story. As you recall and ponder your own stories, I pray that Jesus will touch your heart to see the same thread of love as I have found in my stories. I am praying for you, even though we have never met. I am praying that as you read my stories, you will find true freedom and healing in Jesus in your stories.

In our first snapshot story, four-year-old Rita is on her way to the train station to meet her daddy—or so she thought. She will share her experience.

The Train Station

I am so excited! I am going to the train station to meet my daddy!
I can see the train station! I think I see smoke. That is the train coming. My daddy is on that train. It must be fun to ride on a train. I know that on a train you can hear the whistle blow and see the trees and fields and towns as you fly by. I like trains. My daddy is on a train coming to see me.

I didn't know that I have a daddy. I know that I have a grand-dad. He comes over sometimes at night when my mommy isn't home. I love to sit on his lap and listen to his stories of growing up on a farm. My brother, Tony, and I share his lap and listen to every word of his stories. When he leaves, he always says, "See you in the funny papers." Am I in the funny papers? Who knows? Who cares?

We both laugh and yell back to our granddad, "See you in the funny papers!"

We are at the train station! How will I know my daddy? I don't need to know who he is because my daddy will know me. When Daddy sees me, he will pick me up and take me in his arms and hug me tightly. We will be so happy to see each other. I have a daddy!

Wait! What? What is that? It is a box. Tell me what is going on! A box is not my daddy. My daddy can't be in that box. I want to see my daddy! Where is my daddy?

Doesn't he want to see me? Doesn't he want to hug me? Why didn't my daddy come home to be with me? Why won't anyone talk to me? Doesn't he want me? Why doesn't he want me? Tell me what is going on. "Granddad, talk to me. What is going on?"

6

My dear friend,

So what kind of book of faith, encouragement, and hope starts off with a story of a heartbroken, confused four-year-old girl? The truth is that my story, your story, and everyone's story comes with heartbreak, pain and, sometimes, confusion. There are times in our stories that we ask ourselves, "What is going on? I am confused. What is happening in my life?" What we often don't see or realize is that through our heartbreak and pain, God is, and always has been, right there with us.

Actually, he was with us before we were born. Jeremiah 1:5 tells us, "Before I formed you in the womb I knew you, before you were born I set you apart." In our times of experiencing heartbreak or pain as well as joy and love, God is with us. I do not want to try to explain *why* something happens in my stories or your stories. However, together, we will explore the lessons, joys, and blessings by seeing and acknowledging the truth of *who* is present in our stories.

We never talked about that day again. Years later, I learned that during World War II, my dad drove a tank. He was killed in France in August 1944, six months after I was born. It wasn't until years after the war that some soldiers were brought home to their families for burial.

I do not recall anyone ever talking to me about anything as I was growing up. For that time period, that is not unusual. In the '40s and '50s, when I was growing up, children were not the "center of the universe" in the family dynamics. If a toy was lost or broken, parents would not run out to find a replacement. If I lost or broke something, I had to find it or fix it myself or go without. I certainly would not cry about a lost or broken toy or anything else, for that matter. If I did, I was sure to hear, "Stop crying, or I'll give you something to cry about." It seems that same philosophy applied to hurt feelings or a broken heart. I was left to either fix the heartbreak myself or bury the pain and move on,

It isn't that my family didn't love me. They did. I just don't recall any conversations about my day or theirs. We also didn't have conversations about obedience. If my mom or stepdad said it, we better obey—no discussion or family meeting.

I have seen parents today kneel to the eye level of a child and talk to him or her eyeball to eyeball in very clear language so that there is no confusion about what is being communicated. I love it! Sometimes I wonder if my life story would have been different if someone had knelt down and looked at me eyeball to eyeball and explained all that was happening that day. I say that because somehow, in my little four-year-old mind, I thought that my daddy didn't want to come home to me. I couldn't understand why he didn't want me. Would an eyeball-to-eyeball conversation have changed anything? We will never know.

As a child, my fantasy went something like this: It was all a mistake. My daddy is really alive, living in France until the day he can get home. When he finally does come home, he indeed will pick me up and hold me tightly in his arms. When he comes home, he will be a perfect father, and I will have a wonderful, beautiful life.

As an adult, I carried the belief that if my dad had come home, I would be an emotionally healthy woman with a wonderful husband and perfect kids. I would not be a "messed up" woman. It has been a process letting go of that fantasy.

The truth is that I am becoming the woman that God created me to be. All of my experiences, whether they are hurts, heartbreaks, confusion, or joy, are shaping me into something beautiful. It has only taken me seventy-five years to learn that truth! I am a slow learner. Ha-ha-ha.

My dear friend, I pray that you won't have to live another day believing anything but the truth. You need to know that God is at work in you, creating someone beautiful. That is not a fantasy. It is truth!

Do you have any "what if" or "if only" fantasies? My favorite verse as a teenager was Romans 8:28, "And we know that in all things God works for the good of those who love him, who have been called according to his purpose."

Maybe today is the day to let go of your "what if" or "if only" and walk in his love, knowing that in all things, God is at work for your good. He is creating in you something beautiful

Today, I don't say "What if had a daddy." I do have a daddy. Let me jump a little ahead in my story. As a teenager, I accepted Jesus and became a believer. I was adopted into God's family and became God's child. I have a daddy! Paul tells us in Galatians 4:6, "Because you are his sons, God sent the Spirit of his Son into our hearts, the Spirit who calls out, 'Abba Father.'" Abba, Father, is the intimate way of addressing our heavenly Father, just as daddy is the intimate form of Father.

When I pray, I often cry out to my daddy. What a joy to know that he hears me, loves me, and is here for me at all times, in every situation. In the tough times, painful times, or confusing times, I can go to my daddy, talk to him and see, know, and experience his incredible love in the midst of my pain, heartbreak, or confusion. However, I need to make the choice to approach my daddy daily in prayer.

I need to tell you that there are times that I still want a human rescuer to swoop down, pick me up, and make life all better for me. Dear one, have you been hoping and waiting for a rescuer as well? Trust me, it doesn't work out well to put your faith and hope in anyone other than our Abba, Father. Believe me, I have lived with the expectation that another person could be my *all in all* and rescuer. Living with that expectation from another person is a destructive and unhealthy way to live and relate.

We miss out on such a wonderful relationship when we look to anyone other than our heavenly Daddy to take first place in our lives. He is always there for us, ready to scoop us up in his everlasting arms of love.

Before I came to faith in Jesus as a teenager, God was at work in my heart through Bible stories told to me and my brother by our Uncle Paul. Uncle Paul was a great storyteller. Elementary school aged Rita would love to introduce you to Uncle Paul. As you will see, Uncle Paul is unique.

Uncle Paul

"Let me lie down with the Philistines!" Uncle Paul pushed on the chairs, and they fell down all over him. "Samson died with the evil Philistines," declared Uncle Paul. I squealed with delight.

"Tell us another story. Just one more story, please. I love Bible stories," I pleaded.

I love my Uncle Paul and the Bible stories that he tells me and my brothers Tony and Johnny Wayne. Tony is two years older than me, but we play together and listen to Bible stories together. Our little brother, Johnny Wayne, is only two, but we let him tag along sometimes. He loves Uncle Paul's Bible stories too. We love how Uncle Paul tells Bible stories. He becomes a character in the stories he tells us. We love Uncle Paul.

I am not so sure that my dad likes Uncle Paul. He never looks happy to see him. Uncle Paul is a traveling preacher, so he doesn't get to come see us a lot. We never know when he will come or how long he will stay with us. We kids are always happy to see him. Daddy is never happy to see him, but that doesn't seem to bother Uncle Paul.

Uncle Paul does strange things sometimes, like sleep in his clothes. I thought that it was a good idea to sleep in your clothes, so I tried it. It was a good idea until my dad yelled at me at breakfast.

One time, I asked Uncle Paul why he slept in his clothes. I didn't understand his answer. He said, "I will never take off my pants in another man's home."

"Why?" I asked. "Are you afraid the man will steal your pants?"

"No," he answered.

My brother Tony said that it had something to do with not wanting to be naked around another man's wife. I think it is a good idea not to be naked around anyone. I don't care if Uncle Paul does strange things. I like him and his Bible stories.

I don't know my favorite Bible story. I do know the saddest story is when Jesus was hanging on a cross and died. Uncle Paul says that Jesus died for me to take my punishment for the bad things I do. He did that because he loves me. But that doesn't make sense. He died before I was even born. How could he love me before I was even born?

One time, Tony asked if God is like Santa Claus. "Are adults just making up God?" Tony asked.

Uncle Paul told him that God and Jesus are real. He said that God created everything, including us. His Son Jesus died for us. Jesus came back to life three days after he died on the cross. I want to believe that there is a God and that he made everything and that he loves me. I want to believe that he sent his Son, Jesus, to die for me.

Uncle Paul gave us Bibles one day and said that he would give us five dollars each if we would read the Bible. Wow! That is a lot of money. I opened my Bible and began to read. "In the be... God... er..." Those words were too big for me to read because I am only in second grade. I like it better when Uncle Paul tells us Bible stories.

One day, Uncle Paul asked us if we wanted to go to a church where they had a school called Vacation Bible School.

"Will they tell us Bible stories?" I asked.

"They will," Uncle Paul happily declared. So off we went in Uncle Paul's pickup truck. We were excited to be going to church for the first time.

The teacher told us Bible stories, but she didn't pretend to be a character in the story. It wasn't as much fun as Uncle Paul's Bible stories, but I listened. She told us the story about how Jesus died on the cross and that he became alive after three days, which is why we have Easter. Jesus arose on Easter. I didn't know that Jesus rose on Easter. I thought that Easter was when the Easter bunny came. I learned something new at Vacation Bible School!

The best part was painting. I painted a flower on a piece of wood. It had a Bible verse on it. Bible verses are words that are in the Bible. They are words that we are supposed to learn. I see why they call this school. That is okay. I like to learn and I like school.

My mom and dad don't take us to church. They are just too busy. We have to work at our motel, restaurant, and gas station. It is the Hilltop Motel. Me and Tony help clean, and sometimes, Tony gets to pump gas at the gas station. Mom is the cook, and Dad is the boss.

Sometimes it can be fun working at the Hilltop Motel. The gas station is the most fun.

When Tony gets to pump gas or wash the car windows, he will sometimes let me help. One day, Tony was playing with the hose that you use to put air into car tires. Tony was pulling on the hose. I am not sure what happened, but the next thing I saw was that the air pump was blowing air on the ground, and tiny pieces of rock and dirt were flying into the air and hitting our little brother Johnny Wayne in both of his legs. All three of us were screaming and crying. Mom came and took Johnny Wayne home. She used tweezers to pull out each little piece of rock. I pretty much stayed away from the gas station after that.

I didn't like thinking about that day and how Johnny Wayne had so many tiny rocks in his legs. When I don't like thinking about something, I start thinking about the Bible stories that Uncle Paul told us. I like thinking about how God made everything. I think about my favorite Bible stories. Does God love me? Does he really, truly love me? I hope so. I love God.

My dear friend,

God does love us. He is real. He loves us so much that he sent his Son, Jesus, to die for us. John 3:16 is the first verse that I memorized, "For God so loved the world that he gave his only begotten son, that whosoever believes in him shall not perish, but have everlasting life" (King James Version). He loves us so much and takes delight in blessing us.

My friend Darryl is always talking about how much he is loved by God. He told me that one day, he was crossing the Coleman Bridge and saw a beautiful sunset over the York River.

"It was breathtakingly beautiful," he declared. "God created that sunset just for me."

"Really, Darryl. You think that God created that sunset that day just for you?" I said sarcastically.

"It's true. If I look down and see the most beautiful blade of grass, I know that God created that single blade of grass just for me," he confidently declared.

This guy is either crazy or really conceited, I was thinking to myself. His wife, Gloria, would probably say both. Ha-ha!

Could it be that God loves beauty and that he had me and you in mind at creation? It blows my mind to consider that God had me in mind when he created the heavens and the Earth. The heavens and the Earth are way too broad. Could it be that he had me in mind when he created the beautiful flowers that I enjoy so much or a single blade of grass that I will see and enjoy! What an amazing, wonderful love! What an amazing, wonderful God.

It turns out that Darryl isn't crazy or conceited. God did indeed create the beauty that you enjoy. It is true! God had you in mind when he created all that exists—even that single blade of grass or flower that you see and enjoy. Do you love the beauty of the sunset? How about the sunrise or the ocean? Are the mountains your thing? He created the beauty that you love. He indeed did have you in mind at creation. I wonder if we really are able to grasp the love of God.

Paul wrote to the Ephesians about the love of God.

> So that Christ may dwell in your hearts through faith. And I pray that you, being rooted and established in love, may have the power, together with all the Lord's holy people to grasp how wide and long and high and deep is the love of Christ. (Ephesians 3:17–18)

Grasping, holding onto, and believing that I am loved has been evading me my entire life. It seems that my life theme or motto has been "Will anyone love me? Please love me." I really, really, really hate telling you that. Wait! It is okay to tell you that because God is delivering me from holding on to the false belief that I am not loved. When those moments of doubt do arise in my head, I know to go to Scripture to see and believe truth. I have learned to speak truth into my own heart. He knew me before I was born, he sent his Son to die for me, and he is with me every single day of my life.

I think that so many times, I have missed seeing the love of God that is right in front of me as well as love expressed to me by others. Often, that love is right before my eyes.

We need to pay attention in life, be alert, and see God. When we pay attention, we will see God and his love every single day of our life. We see God's love in his creation as well as in a text or phone call from a friend, the joy of our children, the warmth of our family, and even a smile from a stranger. What we easily miss is seeing God in the midst of our hurt, pain, or disappoint. God is with us in those times as well. We need to pay attention. So many times I have missed seeing God and his love. Pay attention, Rita. Pay attention, my friend.

My next little story could shed a little light as to why I have struggled so much with love. I have held onto the false belief that I am not worthy of love. Shame has had a grip on me.

We are still in Kansas, at the Hilltop Motel, in my next little story. Second grader, Rita will share this story with you.

Quarantined

"Poliomyelitis. Contagious disease in this house. *Quarantined.*"

"So what do you think that sign on the door says, Tony?" I asked.

"I don't know. Those are big words," he replied. "Mom said that there is a sick kid who lives here. I bet those are just adult words that mean 'Sick kid lives here. He is lonely. Come play with him.'"

"I think you are right." *Knock, knock, knock.*

Well, that was how it all started. That was how we met our new friend and his sister. This kid and his sister were so much fun. The kid didn't look sick to us. We played cards, we talked, we laughed. Sometimes, when he felt good, we would sneak him outside to play with us. His mom worked at our restaurant, so we knew when she would be busy. Every day, we were either at the sick kid's house, at the pond playing with frogs and tadpoles, or picking up pop bottles. We turned in the pop bottles at the store to get money.

Wanna hear a funny story? One day, we took a pickle jar with us to the pond. We thought that it would be a great idea to take a few tadpoles home with us so we could watch them turn into frogs. We caught a few tadpoles and carefully put them in our pickle jar. When we got home, Tony said that the tadpoles shouldn't have to live in dirty water. He put clean water in a glass, then carefully caught each tadpole and put them in the glass of water. Not long after our tadpoles were all set in their new home, Dad came home. He saw the glass of water, and before we could stop him, he drank the water and our tadpoles! We didn't know what to do.

"Should I tell him?" I asked Tony.

"Do you want to get a spanking?" he asked.

So we watched Dad. We didn't know if he would die, throw up, or just get a tummy ache. Nothing happened. Absolutely nothing! Dad just acted like his normal self. When we realized that he was okay, we both started laughing.

Wow, I didn't know that you can shallow live tadpoles and not get sick or die. I don't think that I want to try it though.

One day, I went over to the sick kid's house by myself. Tony and I went everywhere together, but this particular day, I wasn't with Tony. I don't know what he was doing. I knocked on the door and our friend answered.

"What do you want to do?" our friend asked me.

"I don't know. Whatever you want to do," I replied.

"Wanna play a game that adults play?" he asked me.

"My mom and dad don't play games," I replied.

"I bet they play this game," he insisted. "Come on, it will be fun," he begged me.

I agreed to play the adult game. The rules were simple. He said that we would play our usual card game, and whoever loses would take off one piece of clothing.

"I'm not so sure I like this game," I told him.

"You are not a baby are you?" he asked.

When it came down to my last piece of clothing, I said I didn't want to play anymore.

I didn't look at him, and I really didn't want him to look at me.

He kept telling me that we had to finish the game and do what the adults do.

"What the adults do is really fun. You want to do what adults do, don't you?" he said. "Don't be a baby."

I took off my panties and tried to cover myself with my hands. I felt sick. I wished that I could leave. *Why am I so bad? This is bad, really bad,* I was thinking.

"Now we will do what adults do," he said.

I remember nothing after that. I don't remember getting dressed or going home. I never saw that kid again. What I do remember is being at home and looking for my music box. I couldn't find my music box. It is round and has a soft beautiful lid with flowers painted on top. When you open the lid, you can hear the music play. I love my music box. I wanted my music box so much. I wanted to hear music play. I couldn't find my music box.

Rescue
By Lauren Daigle

You're are not hidden
There's never been a moment
You were forgotten
You are not hopeless
Though you have been broken
Your innocence stolen

I hear you whisper underneath your breath
I hear your SOS, your SOS

I will send out an army to find you
In the middle of the darkest night
It's true, I will rescue you

Dear friend,

Lauren Daigle is my favorite Christian music artist. My favorite lines from her song "Rescue" declare that God will send out an army to find you in the middle of the darkest night. How cool is that? There is no darkness that is too dark for God to find you and rescue you!

Only God can rescue us from an experience that is so horrific that our brain blocked the memory as a form of protection and self-preservation. Only God can rescue us from the consequences of sin; our sin as well as sins against us, sins thrust upon us in a sinful and fallen world. Only God can rescue our heart and mind!

After the experience of "playing the adult game," I *knew* that I had done something bad. In that moment, I took on the identity of shame. The *Oxford* dictionary's definition of *shame* is "a painful feeling of humiliation or distress caused by the consciousness of wrong or foolish behavior." I believed that I had done something bad and that I was a bad person—a person not worthy of being loved. Shame stole my true identity, so I took on a *false* identity. I started believing a lie about myself. I believed that I was *bad*.

I believed that no one could love a bad child. So as a child and teenager, I found my identity by becoming who others wanted me to be. I could be whoever someone needed me to be. Shame stole my true identity.

After I was married and had children, my new identity became wife and mom. Later in life, I earned my teaching certificate and brand-new identity—*teacher*. Even though my *roles* in life changed and my identity appeared to change, I still carried with me the wounded little girl who believed that she was bad and unworthy of love. That *false identity* that I carried kept me from stepping into the woman that God created me to be.

So as a woman who has lived seventy-six years on this earth, who am I today? In the depth of my soul, am I still that little girl who was "bad"? Am I the little girl who feels unworthy of love?

I do know that little girl still lives deep within. I believe that each of us has our inner child somewhere deep within our heart and mind. The *Oxford* dictionary defines the *inner child* as "a person's supposed original or true self, especially when regarded as damaged or concealed by negative childhood experiences."

Many, many books have been written about healing the child within. For me, my healing comes from knowing Jesus and who he is in my life as well as accepting and becoming the person that he created me to be.

I have found in my life that knowing Jesus and believing all that he says and making his truth real within my life is a journey of love and faith. I must trust Jesus but also believe what he says about who I am as his child. I have never had any trouble believing that "God so loved the world" or that he loves you. You are probably awesome; me, however, not so much. How could he love me? Doesn't he know that I am the bad girl?

Praise Jesus that I don't need to live wondering who I am. I can claim my true identity in him! My identity is found in knowing the one to whom I belong. I belong to the one who rescues me in the middle of the night when I feel alone, worthless, and insecure. I belong to the one who sees me, knows me, and loves me. I am God's dearly loved child.

> Christ forgave you. Follow God's example therefore, as dearly loved children. And walk in the way of love just as Christ loves us and gave himself up for us as a fragrant offering and sacrifice to God." (Ephesians 5:1–2)

My true identity is found only in my relationship with God through Jesus Christ.

It is in those intimate times in prayer that I am assured that I am valued, treasured, and loved by God. For me it is a decision that I need to make every single day to believe Jesus and who he says that I am. I decide every single day whether I will believe the lies of Satan, who tells me that I am bad and unworthy, or the truth that God says to me that I am chosen, set apart, loved, and his dearly loved child.

Stepping into the woman that God created me to be is a journey of love with Jesus.

What is your true identity? Are you living with shame that you have carried for a lifetime? Are you living with a false identity? Maybe someone told you that you are not enough or maybe too much. Maybe you have told yourself that you are "bad or unworthy or not enough." Whether we put the lie on ourselves or are lied to by others, the source of the lie is Satan. John 10:10 tells us, "The thief comes only to steal and kill and destroy; I have come that they may have life, and have it to the full."

May I suggest something? I suggest that you go to the feet of Jesus right now. Ask Jesus to reveal any shame that you have been carrying that has robbed you of knowing and living in your true identity; that woman that God created you to be. Who does Jesus say you are?

I pray for you that you will embrace your true identity as his beloved child. I also pray that daily, we will truly know, see, and grasp his incredible love for us. Allow Jesus to rescue you from the pain of shame. Remember that he is here, ready to rescue you.

> So do not fear, for I am with you: do not be
> dismayed, for I am your God. I will strengthen
> you and help you: I will uphold you with my
> righteous hand. (Isaiah 4:10)

Even though we have not met, I am praying for you. If you are reading these words, know that you are so loved and that I am praying for you even as I write.

My friend, my next story takes us to 1955 in Orange County, California! Are you ready to read about the boom years of California? These were the best years of my life. Rita, as a teenager, will share with you the adventures of moving to California.

California

California is awesome! It doesn't look at all like Kansas. You would have to see it to believe it! Everywhere you look, you see strawberry fields, orange groves, palm trees and, best of all, beaches—lots of beaches! The ones I know about are Redondo Beach, Long Beach, Huntington Beach, and Newport Beach. Redondo Beach is so much fun. At night, the pier is lit up, and it feels like excitement is in the air. Balboa Island has a ferry that is really cool. My dad took us on a ferry ride just for fun. My favorite beach is Newport Beach. There are a lot of surfers at Newport Beach. I like watching the surfers.

I think that the best time to go the beach is at night. The air is cool, salty, damp, and so amazing. The fires at the beach at night are so cool! I don't like the hot, crowded daytime beach. I lay on a towel a couple of times, but it was not fun for me. I was hot, sandy, and sunburned. Not fun at all. I would much rather body surf or walk on the beach at night or simply sit by the fire.

The first beach we went to was Redondo Beach. My aunt lives in Redondo Beach, so we stayed with her when we first got to California. I love her house. On both sides of the sidewalk going to her house, there are strawberries. Strawberries in the front yard! So amazing and so tasty!

Orange trees are in the front yard too! Who would plant orange trees in the front yard?

I grew radishes once in Kansas but never strawberries or oranges. I don't even like radishes, but my dad said that they grow quickly, so I planted a patch of radishes. My dad ate them. I wish that I had grown strawberries.

Sometimes my brothers and I liked to go outside, not to play but to eat! There really isn't a place to play in her yard. I can't believe how small the yards are in California. They are not big enough to ride a bike.

The sad part of California yards is that they do not have ponds. However, there are beaches in California. Sometimes, Tony and I would walk to the beach. With our pockets filled with fruit, off to the beach we would go.

Have you ever heard of a grunion run? Late at night, tiny silver fish called grunion "run" up from the ocean on to the beach. It is crazy amazing. During a full moon, the tiny fish come on the beach with the waves. The female grunion makes a hole in the sand with her tail and then lays eggs. Then the male will go to the holes and fertilize the eggs. After all this, they wiggle off the sand back into the ocean.

We never know when or what time the grunion run, so we sometimes go to the beach and wait and hope that we get to see them coming in with the waves. Sometimes we go to see a grunion run, and they don't show up.

The beaches are amazing, but there is so much more to see and do in California.

My dad took us to Hollywood to see where movie stars have their handprints on the sidewalk. I saw Abbott and Costello's handprints, Roy Rogers and his horse, Trigger, and John Wayne. My mom and dad love John Wayne!

My mom and dad got to go to a game show that was in a television studio. The game show was shown later on television. Mom won a watch! We kids didn't get to go, but we were excited that Mom won a watch.

We could have taken a bus ride to see the homes of movie stars, but my dad said that was the dumbest idea he had ever heard. "Why am I going to give my money to someone just to take me to look at the outside of a house?" Dad yelled. So we just rode around.

We went to the corner of Hollywood and Vine. It is supposed to be a famous spot, but it looked normal to me. Maybe Dad was right after all.

Our family looked at a lot of houses when we first came to California. Most of the houses looked exactly alike. Maybe the garage was on a different side, but the inside of the houses were all the same. It really didn't matter to us that they were the same because all the houses were brand-new. They were big pretty houses. The yards weren't big though, which meant there was no place to ride my bike, explore, or play in a pond. We finally found the perfect house for us.

Our house has four bedrooms! I have my own room. Tony has a room that he shares with Granddad when he comes to visit. Johnny Wayne has his own room too. Of course, my mom and dad share a room. Our house is so pretty and big. We also have a big television in our house.

There aren't any fun things to play outside here, except tetherball. Dad put in a pole in the backyard so that we can play tether ball. We play sometimes, but it got boring after a while.

Dad bought a big television for us to watch. Sometimes we even eat while watching our television shows. When I come home from school, I watch *Mickey Mouse Club* and *American Bandstand* on our big television.

Annette and Tommy are my favorite Mouseketeers. The Mouseketeers always start the show by dancing. Then we get to see a cartoon or the *Adventures of Spin and Marty*. I love every moment of the *Mickey Mouse Club*.

My favorite cartoons are the *Donald Duck Cartoons*. Donald gets mad sometimes and then jumps up and down making noises, like maybe he is cussing. So funny! My favorite *Donald Duck Cartoons* are the ones with the squirrel and also the ones with the bees.

Donald plays tricks on the squirrels, Chip and Dale. The squirrels always win in the end. Donald is no match for the clever bees. They, too, win in the end.

Jimmy, the host, will end the show by singing a song and saying, "See you real soon. Why? Because we like you!" That is so funny and awesome! It always makes me laugh when Jimmy says that he likes us!

American Bandstand has the best music ever. The guests on the show are the same people that we listen to on Tony's radio. I watch very closely how they dance on *Bandstand*. One day, I said to myself,

"Hey, I can do that too!" You twist your foot on your toe, then kick your foot back, then do the same of the other foot. It is so much fun to dance. Tony and Johnny Wayne won't dance with me, so I dance by myself. Dancing is so much fun!

I don't have a radio, so I listen to Tony's. My favorite singers are Elvis Presley, the Chordettes, the Platters, and Bill Haley. The first rock and roll song that I ever heard was "Rock Around the Clock" by Bill Haley and the Comets. "Shake, Rattle, and Roll" is also my favorite. Those songs are so much better than the country music that my parents listen to.

One day, we heard on Tony's radio that our station was going to have a contest between all the schools in Orange County. The school that had the most kids who call the radio station would get a sock hop brought to their school. All we had to do was give out the phone number of the station to everyone at school and get them to call the radio station. I wrote out the phone number on tiny pieces of paper and gave it to all the kids in my class. Then they gave out the number to other kids. Our school won!

We got a real dance at our school! They brought a man who played records that we could hear on a big speaker. They even brought stuff for us to eat and drink. The sock hop was so much better than I thought it would be!

The best part of the dance was when I was dancing with Jim. I saw some girls watching us dance. They were sorta' moving their feet just like I was. They were watching me dance! Don't they watch *Bandstand?* I guess they don't watch it like I do. If they watched *American Bandstand*, they could learn how to bop. They probably would not be as good as me though.

Did I tell you that I have a boyfriend? His name is Jim. Jim isn't the first boy that I have liked, but he is the first boy who likes me back. I love how he combs his hair. He parts it on the side and then pulls one side up so that it makes a big wave. I think that he gets his hair to stand up by using hair cream. Tony uses hair cream too. One guy I saw used too much hair cream and, boy, did he look greasy! My cheek actually felt greasy after I danced with one guy. I guess guys gotta be careful about how much hair cream they use.

I went to a party not long ago. We played spin the bottle. The way that we played the game was that we would sit in a circle. Someone would spin a bottle. The person spinning would have to kiss the person that the bottle pointed to after the spin. The good thing is that we didn't have to kiss in front of everyone. After the spin, the two people would have to go into the clothes closet to kiss. My spin happened to land on a boy who I didn't like all that much. We went into the closet and stood there for a while and then came out. We pretended that we had kissed. Everyone thought that we were so cool because we stayed in the closet a long time.

Just like in Kansas, Tony always had good ideas for us to have fun. One day, after it started to get dark, he told me about a really fun way to play a joke on our neighbors.

First, we made sure that our neighbors had their lights on in the house. Then we went to the back of the house and found a special little door that opened up to switches. Tony then showed me how to flip the switches, and the lights would go out in the house. Then we could hear our neighbors yelling and asking what happened. Then he switched the lights back on. We could hear them talking again. After a minute or two, he turned the lights off again. The dad started yelling and cussing. This time, I didn't think it was so funny, so I ran. I didn't want to get into trouble. Tony thought it was so funny that I ran. He said that watching me run was as much fun as turning the lights off and on.

There was a better joke that we played on someone that didn't scare me so much. Let me tell you what happened. When it was starting to get dark outside, Tony asked me to go inside our house and get all our toilet paper rolls.

"All of them?" I asked.

"Yes, we need lots of toilet paper. Go get every roll in every bathroom and then check the hall closet," he ordered.

So off I went and got all the toilet paper that I could find. I did just like he said. I took every roll out of our three bathrooms and then checked the hall closet for more rolls. My arms were full of toilet paper, so full that I kept dropping them and then picking them up!

We walked a block over to his girlfriend's house. We took all of the toilet paper rolls and unrolled the paper on the trees, the flowers, the rose bushes and even the cars. We used almost every single roll. Toilet paper was everywhere! After we were finished, we stood back and looked at our masterpiece. We laughed so hard, I had tears coming down my cheeks.

I don't know which was more fun, toilet papering a house or just hanging out with my big brother, Tony. I wish that we could have seen his girlfriend's face when she saw her toilet-papered yard. Later, she told Tony that she thought it was funny, but her dad was really mad. Tony always has great ideas for having fun. His friends were fun too.

Once in a while, Tony and his friends like to shoot baskets in front of our house. We have a hoop over the garage door. One day, before Tony went out with his friends, they let me shoot baskets with them. They are such cool guys.

I like how they dress. They usually wear white T-shirts and blue jeans. They sometimes wear their hair slicked back. Sometimes they put cigarette packages in their sleeves. I don't think Tony smokes, but sometimes he has cigarettes tucked into his T-shirt. My brother Tony is so awesome. He gets me into trouble sometimes, but he is a great brother.

I love California. I don't miss the pond and fields so much anymore. On my way to school, I walk by orange groves. The flowers are beautiful before they turn into oranges. I like staying inside sometimes and watching television too. I love my friends and being in junior high. I am making good grades. I got all As on my report card. I also like the fun stuff Tony finds for us to do. I am happy that we moved to California. It is a good place to live.

Dear friend,

Do you have a favorite year or years—maybe a decade? The best years ever for me were 1955–1956—the innocence, wonder, and excitement of the '50s! People were migrating to California in the early '50s in search of a better life. The early '50s brought us the expansion of McDonalds, the opening of Disneyland, the popularity of rock and roll, the bop, sock hops, the movies of James Dean and Marilyn Monroe, the music and movies of Elvis Presley as well as my favorite TV shows—*Leave It to Beaver*, *Mickey Mouse Club*, and *American Bandstand*. That is a very short list of all that was new and exciting in the '50s.

I wish that I could hear your favorite stories of your younger years, the games you played, your favorite TV show or movie, your favorite place to live, and your favorite relative. I know that I would love your stories—stories that bring a smile to your face and joy to your heart. It is good to remember—remember times spent with family, times of joy in solitude, and times of enjoying the life that God has given us.

Are you building memories for your children? Special holiday trips, special family traditions or special times at home all work together to provide memories for you to treasure together.

A special memory for me as an adult is the mission trip to Honduras that my daughter Lori and grandson Johnathan and I took together. What an amazing trip it was. I also treasure the memory of the special times together while camping through Europe with my then husband Ed and my daughter Kristy. Seems like everyone that we saw stopped to tell me how beautiful Kristy was. My little girl with pigtails looked like she belonged in Germany.

Oh, and there was the trip by bus from the East Coast to the West Coast with my girls. The girls were very little and the trip had its tiring moments, funny moments, and even a dangerous moment. What was I thinking, taking my very young daughters from Virginia to California by bus! I don't know, but it sure was fun!

Memories! What fun it is to look back on our shared memories with those we love. No one can steal those moments of pure joy from our hearts—not distance, not time, not death, or even strained present relationships.

You know what else that we need to reflect on and remember? It is those times of God's blessings, deliverance and presence.

> I remember the days of long; I meditate
> on all your works and consider what your hands
> have done. I spread out my hands to you; I thirst
> for you like a parched land. God is always faithful
> to us. (Psalm 143:5)

Do you remember how he has been faithful to you? I love the lines from the Lauren Daigle song "I Remember."

> I remember, I remember
> You have always been faithful to me
> I remember, I remember
> Even when my own eyes could not see
> You were there, always there.

When the dark clouds or storms of life hit us, we will need to remember those times of the faithfulness of God toward us. Have you read the stories of the Israelites? God delivered them from slavery, parted the Red Sea, and delivered them through the wilderness. Yet they forgot God's faithfulness. They questioned God, "Did you deliver us from our enemies so that we could starve in the wilderness?" I wonder, at the first sign of trouble, do we remember.? "I remember, I remember / Even when my own eyes could not see / You were there, always there."

"Thank you, Jesus, for being there, always there for me. Thank you for your constant love in good times as well as difficult times. Lord, remind me when I forget that you are there, always there with me. I love you. Amen."

My next story takes us to the most difficult time of my life. I was in the seventh grade when I answered the phone and heard words that would change my life forever.

Life and Death

"It's time!" declared Mom.

"What? Time for what?" I asked my mom.

"It is time for me to have my baby. The baby is coming." excitedly declared Mom.

I was so excited to see our new baby. I wanted our baby to be a girl. Two brothers are enough. I love Tony and Johnny Wayne, but I need a sister.

"I am so excited," I shouted. "It's time. It is time!"

Raelene Annette was born December 23, 1956, the best day of my life so far. I was so excited to meet my new sister. Dad and Granddad wouldn't let us kids go to the hospital to see Mom and Raelene. Dad said that kids are not allowed in hospitals unless they are sick. We waited days before we got to meet our new sister.

Finally, our car drove up. Me, Tony, and Johnny Wayne ran out to meet our new sister.

"What is her name?" I excitedly asked Mom.

"Raelene Annette," Mom proudly declared.

Raelene is such a pretty name. Annette is the perfect middle name. Annette Funicello is my favorite Mouseketeer. Raelene has the same name as a *Mickey Mouse Club* Mouseketeer! I love it!

Mom had Raelene snuggly wrapped in a blanket. We were so excited to get inside and take the blanket off of her so that we could see our new baby sister. Once inside, me, Tony, and Johnny Wayne crowded around Raelene and just stared. She was so beautiful!

"She doesn't have any hair," laughed Tony. "Even without hair, she is beautiful!"

We all agreed. Mom said that I could hold her. Raelene was so tiny. I loved holding her and looking at my new baby sister, Raelene Annette. I finally had a sister, not just a plain ole' normal sister but a beautiful, wonderful sister. I loved saying her name, Raelene Annette.

As I held Raelene, I thought about all the good times that we would have playing together. I was excited to take her to Disneyland. I knew that she would love Fantasyland. I bet Dumbo will be her favorite ride. I still have tickets that are good for the rides in Fantasyland. When Mom has to go out someplace, I could be the babysitter. Having a sister will be so much better than brothers because I know that Raelene won't hit me or tease me! I can't believe it! I was so excited to have a beautiful sister!

We had a great Christmas with our new sister. Mom bought gifts for her that she couldn't open. The best gift for all of us that year was Raelene Annette. New Year's Eve, we stayed up late and talked about how much fun our new year would be.

On January 4, 1957, the phone rang. No one seemed to be around, so I answered it. The person on the other end asked if Tony Kelso lived there. I said that he did, but he was not home. The person on the other end asked to speak to an adult, so I gave the phone to my mom. After Mom hung up, she told us that Tony was in the hospital. He was in a car accident. Mom told me to hold Raelene if she woke up, and then they hurried out the door. Shortly, a neighbor came over to stay with us kids while Dad, Mom, and Granddad were at the hospital.

I immediately went to my bedroom and knelt by my bed and asked God to let my brother live. "Please don't let Tony die," I begged God. After I prayed, I waited in my bedroom for Mom, Dad, Tony, and Granddad to come home.

As I sat on my bed praying, Granddad came into my room.

"He's gone," Granddad said, crying.

"Tony is gone? What do you mean gone? Did Tony die" I demanded to know.

Granddad explained what happened. He said that Tony was alive when they got to the hospital. Tony said that the brakes on the car wouldn't work. He said that he pushed the brakes to the floor, but the car kept going.

Then Tony told them that he was thirsty, but the doctor could not give him anything to drink because his chest hit the steering wheel and was injured. They were going to take him to surgery. Then Tony just stopped breathing.

"He is gone," Granddad said again.

Granddad gave me a quick hug and walked out of my room.

I stayed in my room all the next day. All I wanted was to be left alone. I didn't cry. I didn't want to talk to anyone. I didn't feel like eating either. I just wanted to be by myself.

Mom finally insisted that I come out of my room to eat. At the dinner table, my dad explained that Tony was driving in the rain, and he must have gone through deep water because he had both the clutch and the brake pushed all the way to the floorboard when the police came. He couldn't stop at the stop sign and hit a telephone pole. Dad explained that when the brakes on a car get wet in a puddle, the driver should pump them. He said that brakes should be pumped when going through the water.

I wondered why no one told Tony that. Did he know that? It is not his fault.

"Dad, why didn't you tell Tony to pump his brakes when they got wet? Shouldn't you have told him that? Why didn't anyone tell Tony what to do? It is not his fault that he is dead."

I went back to my room and began crying out to God. I told him that I was mad at him for not letting Tony live. I was mad at my dad for not telling Tony what to do when the brakes get wet.

I was mad at Tony too. Why did he get in a car and drive when it was raining outside? Not only that. Why did he drive a car at all? This isn't Kansas. Uncle Paul let us kids drive his pickup truck on country roads in Kansas. Driving in California isn't like driving on a country road. Tony did not have a license. He should not have been driving at all.

I couldn't stop myself from asking questions. Why did Tony drive that night? Was he going to a party? Was he going to see his girlfriend? All these questions and thoughts made me mad, sad, and hurt. I was mad at everything and everyone. I decided to stay in my room and read. I was too mad and too sad to talk to anyone.

Some friends came over from school. Mom made me leave my room to go talk to them. They said that they were sorry that my brother died. They asked me if I wanted to come outside or go watch television with them. I said that I didn't. So after they left, I went back to my room.

Mom said that we had to take Tony back home to Kansas to be buried. Granddad agreed. He said that he would pay for the train tickets for us to go back to Kansas so we could take Tony to be buried next to our real dad, Tommy. Mom said that she couldn't travel right now with our baby sister, so Uncle Paul came to stay with her.

You remember my Uncle Paul, right? He is the one who told us the cool Bible stories.

My dad seemed happy that Uncle Paul came to stay with Mom. Maybe Dad does like Uncle Paul. I hope he does.

At the funeral home in Kansas, they opened the casket for us to see Tony. That was a terrible idea. When Aunt Blendena saw him, she cried, "That is not Tony Gene. It can't be Tony Gene."

I didn't want to, but I looked into the casket. It was Tony all right.

"What did they do to his hair? He would never comb his hair like that. What the heck! He is wearing a suit. Who put a suit on my brother?"

I thought to myself, *Man, he would be mad if he knew they did this to him. He would never wear a suit. Is he in heaven seeing all this? If he is, I bet he is mad. Is someone going to put a dress on me when I die? They better not.*

Uncle Paul told us all about heaven and hell.

I prayed to God, "God, please let Tony be in heaven with you. I know he really believes that you are real and not like Santa Claus. I know that he was cool and tried to be tough sometimes, but I know that he loves you, just like I do. I'm not mad anymore. I love you, God. It is not anyone's fault that Tony died. Please God, let Tony be with you in heaven. Amen."

I am so glad that Uncle Paul stayed with Mom and Raelene when we took Tony home to Kansas. He was good like that, to show up at the right time to be helpful. He knew that my family didn't have a lot of money, so he had a great idea on how he could help out.

He took everything out of the refrigerator—mustard, ketchup, hot sauce, jelly, milk, tea, peanut butter, and leftovers. He lined everything up neatly on the countertop. Then he got a big pitcher of water and began filling the containers with the water.

"What are you doing" yelled Mom.

"I am saving you money," he proudly replied. "I am making everything last longer," he declared.

That's my Uncle Paul, always trying to help. Mom did not appreciate his help at all!

Later, as Mom told us that story, she laughed. However, she said that it wasn't funny when it happened. My mom loves Uncle Paul just as much as I do.

Dear friend,

When we first moved to California, I went on a roller coaster at the Long Beach Pike. I had never seen a roller coaster. It looked fun, and everyone else was going to ride, so I thought it was a good idea to ride too. It was fun at first. We slowly climbed up, and I could see the beauty of the Pacific as we went over the water. The view at the top of the coaster was awesome, for a brief second.

Whoosh. Down we went. My stomach felt like it moved. It was in my throat. The coaster made a quick turn over the water. I felt like we were going to fall into the Pacific where I would die. Then the coaster seemed fun again. There were a few fast turns but not too scary. I thought to myself, *This is not so bad.*

Whoosh! Down again we went. Again my stomach was in my throat! My heart, on the other hand, was sinking. I was scared. I kept thinking, *When will this ride end? My insides are a mess. I think that I am going to throw up.* I hate roller coasters!

That was what life felt like for me the summer of 1955 through the beginning of 1957—a roller-coaster ride. I loved moving to California. I had friends, a great home, straight As in school and, best of all, a baby sister. I was so excited to get to experience the best day of my life so far when Raelene was born. Life was great for a while. Little did I know that the big "whoosh" was on its way.

Tony went out on a rainy night. His brakes got wet. He died. *Whoosh!* Down I went! My stomach moved into my throat, and my heart sank. My insides were a mess.

The trip to Kansas was bittersweet. I got to see my family. I really missed my cousins especially. I felt so happy the days that we were in Kansas. My cousin Yvonne kissed me so much and hugged me so many times. I so much needed the mothering that she provided for me. Finally, I was beginning to feel *better.* Life was beginning to look good again. I didn't have a desire to be alone. I wanted to be with my family in Kansas. I missed Mom and Raelene but loved being with my Kansas family so much as well. I actually thought that I would be happy again. Wait, here it comes…

Whoosh! The roller coaster fell again when my granddad said he wouldn't be coming back to California with us. He wanted to stay in Kansas. There goes my stomach again. I felt like I was going to throw up. I begged Granddad to come back home with us, but he said that he needed to stay with Aunt Blendena and my cousins, Yvonne and Jimmy. My heart cried out, *What about me? Don't you love me?*

Whoosh! Down I go again.

Think about it. Isn't life sorta' like a roller-coaster ride? You go on a great vacation or have an amazing time with your family. Then whoosh, you have to come home again to work or school and life. You get a little ahead on that savings account that you have been building. Then whoosh, the dryer breaks. You know how it goes.

Praise Jesus, we are not on a scary big roller-coaster ride all the time, every day.

However, life does have ups, downs, joy, heartbreak, happiness, and pain. What so often happens is that after the whoosh or fall, we can find ourselves lost in the wilderness or wasteland alone. Trust me, I know. Alone is never a good place to be.

Imagine for a minute that you just experienced a big whoosh—the kind of whoosh that makes your stomach feel like you will throw up. Maybe it causes your heart to sink. It could be that a loved one died or you lost your job or perhaps the test results weren't what you expected. Whoosh, down you go. You find yourself in a wasteland of emotion.

So you crawl into bed, cover up your head, and cry. In the midst of your pain, crying and isolation is the exact place that you will find Jesus waiting to hold you, comfort you, strengthen you, and rescue you. Isaiah 43:19 tells us, "See, I am doing a new thing! Now it springs up; do you not perceive it? I am making a way in the wilderness and streams in the wasteland."

The beautiful truth is that Jesus is waiting to meet you wherever you are right now.

You can meet Jesus in church through the word spoken from the pastor or worship songs you sing. You can meet Jesus in your home or daily life. You can meet Jesus in the midst of your deepest sorrow or greatest pain. Jesus is there in your big *whoosh* in your wasteland. You might think that you are alone in the middle of the night, but you are not. You know what else? Jesus is right there with you in your greatest joy and blessing! He is the one who provided your great joy and blessing.

I am praying for you as I write these words. I am praying that as you read, you will open your arms to Jesus right now and surrender all of who you are to all of who he is. I am doing that right now myself.

"Jesus, I praise you for who you are in my life. I love you. I surrender all of who I am to all of who you are. I surrender every situation and every person in my life to you right now. Jesus, I praise you for being right there with me in my joys as well as my sorrows. I love you."

Come with me as I come to Jesus and ask him to come into my life. My next story begins around a year after Tony died. Two men knocked on our door and invited us to come see something unusual at church. Rita, as a teenager, will share with you what happened at church.

Jesus

There was a knock on the door. I ran to the door to find two men. "Mom, two men are here," I yelled.

"Don't let them in. Wait till I get there," she yelled back.

When she came to the door, they introduced themselves as men from Village Bible Church.

"Come in," she offered.

I didn't know what church people look like, but there was something about these church people that I liked. One of the men said that he was the pastor of the church, and the other said that he was an evangelist preacher. Now that caught my attention.

"My Uncle Paul goes to different churches too. He is an evangelist preacher too," I proudly proclaimed.

They were friendly and talked to me like what I had to say was important. They asked me about school and about stuff I like to talk about, like what I do to have fun. I told them that the most fun I had was doing stuff with Tony when he was alive. I told them that Tony died. I think that was the first time I had talked about him since the funeral in Kansas.

They talked to Mom too. They told her that they were having special meetings all week at church. The evangelist said that he would be drawing special pictures using chalk. He showed us one of his drawings. It was so cool. It was a picture of a beautiful flower garden. There was a person in the garden. It looked like he was on his knees. It was really cool.

"Can we go, Momma, please? I wanna watch him draw chalk pictures."

"Okay, we will come," Mom said at last.

The church meeting thing was fun. The man drew the chalk pictures with colored chalk, not the kind of chalk they use at school but special colored chalk. Then he put the chalk pictures on different holders and shined a special light on them. Wow! I loved it.

While he was drawing, he told us about Jesus. I remember hearing about Jesus when we lived at Hilltop Motel in Kansas. Jesus was born on Christmas. Then some people killed him, and he came back to life on Easter. I remember the Jesus stories.

As he drew, he told us that Jesus died for our sins. Then he came back to life three days later. The bad stuff we do is called sin. I didn't know that. I know I do bad stuff sometimes, but I didn't know that it was called sin. People who sin go to hell. Hell is where the devil lives in fire. I don't want to go to hell.

I remember my grandma telling us all about hell and all the things we do that will get us sent to hell when we die. She said that we shouldn't be reading comic books or going to movies or playing cards. Dancing is a really big way to get sent to hell. Mom knows how to dance. Uncle Paul said once that when she was younger, Mom could "cut a rug." Grandma also said that if we skate, we will roller skate right into hell. My grandma sure knows a lot about hell and how to get sent there.

Anyway, the evangelist guy asked us where we would spend eternity when we die—heaven or hell. I thought about Tony. I wondered if he was in heaven or hell. I asked God to take him to heaven. I hope Tony is in heaven. I know when I die that I want to go to heaven, not hell.

The preacher asked us to raise our hand if we want to ask Jesus in our heart and live with him forever. I put my hand up right away. Then we sang a song. The preacher said that we should come to the front of the church if we want Jesus in our heart. I went up there really fast. Mom and Johnny Wayne went to the front of the church too.

Our dad didn't come with us to church. He said that because his dad was a preacher, he spent all his life in church, and he doesn't need to go ever again. I guess he knows all about heaven and hell. Raelene was too little to come to church, so she stayed home with Dad. I will tell her all about heaven and hell later.

After we went to the front of the church, other people came up too. After everyone sang for a while, some church people took me, Mom, and Johnny Wayne to different rooms.

A really nice, pretty woman took me to a small table in a small room. She asked me why I came to the front of the church.

"I want to go to heaven someday." I told her.

She smiled and opened her Bible. She showed me a bunch of different verses as she talked. Verses are what they call words in the Bible. I guess I looked confused, so she closed her Bible and talked to me about sin and death and Jesus.

She told me that God says the punishment for our sins is death. God sent his Son to come to earth to take the punishment for our sins. So it turns out that all the bad stuff that happened to Jesus was because he loves us and took our punishment. After he was beaten and put on the cross, he died. He didn't stay dead. God raised Jesus from the dead on Easter Sunday. The way she told the story made sense to me.

The pretty woman asked me if I wanted to pray and ask Jesus to come into my heart and life. Of course I did. She told me the words to pray. I asked Jesus to forgive me of my sins and to come into my heart. I felt so happy after I prayed. I could hardly wait to see if Mom and Johnny Wayne prayed the same prayer that I did. I found out later that they did.

Dear friend,

Mom, Johnny Wayne, and I were "saved" that day in a small Bible-believing church. The chalk drawings got us to church, but the love of Jesus as well as the love we felt from the people of the church was why we decided to join Village Bible Church.

With the death of Tony, I was acutely aware that anyone can die at any time. The fragileness of life was real to me. Since I sometimes wondered if Tony was in heaven with God, I wanted to do all that I needed to do to know for sure that I would go to heaven someday.

I understood sin and Jesus dying for my sin; however, the *real* motivator of getting "saved" that day was to know for sure where I would go when I died. I did not fully comprehend all that is mine in Christ. I did not know that I am totally and completely loved by Jesus. I knew that he loved the world but did not give much thought to how much he loved me personally. I did not know that he formed me in my mother's womb. Even though I was ignorant to all that was mine in Christ, my journey of love began the day that I asked for forgiveness for my sins and asked Jesus to "come into my heart."

What is amazing and wonderful to me is that even though I did not fully grasp the fullness of the gospel, Jesus met me where I was, and we began our journey together.

I loved going to Sunday school and youth group. I was a little nervous at first because I expected the other kids to be perfect and not sin. Wow, was I in for a surprise. They were "normal" kids just like me. What a relief. I wasn't looking forward to being perfect all the time.

Mr. Plumber was our youth group leader. He taught us how to read and study our Bible. He said that every morning, we should read one chapter in the Bible. After we read, then we should write in a notebook any promises or commands we saw in the chapter and then write what God said to us personally. After we read, he said that we should pray to God just like he is a normal person. I am so grateful to Mr. Plumber. He taught me the value and importance of reading my Bible every day with a notebook, ready to write God's promises, commands, and personal words to me.

In church, we kids were probably not as attentive as we needed to be. We often wrote notes, talked, and laughed during church. Sometimes we would see Mr. Plumber look at us, so we pretended to listen.

Probably one of the greatest lessons I learned early on at Village Bible was to tithe. I got an allowance every week from my parents. I do not recall how much they gave me, but I remember putting twenty-five cents into an envelope every Sunday and putting it into the offering plate. I also collected pop bottles and tithed on that money as well.

It is with fondness that I remember my teenage years spent in church. Since the social life of families took place at church, the church was a second home to us. Most of my friends were at my church. Our youth group met at the church and sometimes in different homes. We played games, listened to Mr. Plumber teach us about Jesus, and hung out together. We did not have big outreach programs or huge events intended to draw in large crowds. I suppose the biggest outreach was the chalk-drawing evangelist. We were encouraged to invite our friends to everything we did together, and the youth group slowly grew.

There were times that we did fun stuff together outside of church. One time, we went to the Orange County Fair together as a youth group. We had so much fun! We paired up to ride some of the rides. The best part of that trip for me was when one of the boys in the group held my hand on one of the rides. Life was simple and joyful during those times of being with the youth group at Village Bible Church.

Sometime later after we joined Village Bible, my brother, Johnny Wayne, told me about a tent church near the beach. It was called the hippie church because a lot of kids attended church barefoot, wearing shorts. Johnny Wayne was one of those barefoot surfers who checked out the tent church. Sometimes they were referred to as the Jesus People. Everyone was welcome. Chuck Smith and a small group started Calvary Chapel in Costa Mesa. Young people flocked to the welcoming church.

With the beginning of Calvary Chapel, I believe that the way we "do church" changed forever. I, too, visited Calvary Chapel and loved the new joyful praise songs as well as the relaxed, friendly atmosphere of the church. I loved the praise music. Many churches did change and move with the times. I believe the music and style of worship of today has its roots in the music and style of Calvary Chapel and the Jesus people.

The church service and "language" spoken in the typical church of today is so different from my teenage years. We no longer use the term "get saved" or asking Jesus to "come into your heart." Obviously, the music has changed. However, what remains the same today and forever is the fact that we, as believers in Jesus, are the church. We, as Christians, are Jesus to others. We are love. We are the love of Jesus to a dying and lost world.

I am so grateful for the church of my teenage years as well as the church where I worship today. Sometimes, I feel like we "bash" the traditional church too much. I know that it is true that many people have wounds stemming from their experiences in the traditional church. I get that. However, for me, the traditional church gave me a solid foundation for my spiritual journey. Whether we worship in a traditional church, someone's home, or a tent, we are all the body of Christ. We are his people, and he is our Savior, Lord, and Lover of our souls.

Do you remember your high school years with fondness? Were they fun years, or not so much? Rita, as a teenager, would love to share with you a brief snapshot of a typical high school conversation.

High School

"Did you guys see that new math sub? What a dream boat!" declared Sandy. "He has the most amazing goatee. How can I do math when he just stands there looking gorgeous?"

"Today he looked at me and asked me a question. I don't know what I said. I could barely speak," I laughed.

"A bunch of nothing is what you said. He asked you if you did your homework, and you told him that math is your favorite subject and that you are going to teach math someday," laughed Cheryl.

'No, I didn't."

"Yes, you did."

"I love his water pants," I dreamily said. "Actually, I like everything about him. I was flunking the class. Now I am getting all As. I wouldn't want Mr. G to think that I am dumb or anything like that."

"Rita, there is nothing dumb about you," Cheryl kindly said.

Brenda chimed into the conversation, changing the subject. "I know a new way to make our hair look totally cool. It is called ratting. It is so easy. First you pull up a section of your hair and comb it backward. Then it will stick up really high. Then when you have all your hair ratted, you smooth it down just a little. The last step is Aqua Net hairspray, lots and lots of hairspray so the style lasts all day."

"How do you get your comb through all those rats out at the end of the day?" I asked.

"That is the hard part," she said. "I washed my hair just like it was, with the rats, and then I couldn't get my comb through my hair."

"Brilliant," laughed Cheryl.

"Rita, I gotta tell you something," Brenda said cautiously. "You probably don't know this, but your boobs are sorta' big. Some of us don't even have boobs, and here you are with these giant boobs."

"Thanks for pointing that out," I said defensively.

"Well, when you sit at the lunch table, sometimes your boobs rest on the table because you are short. Don't do that. It looks sorta' weird."

"I know," I replied. "I forget sometimes. I hate having boobs."

"Why? "asked Sandy. "Boys like boobs and butts. You are lucky to have big boobs. No butt, but at least, you have big boobs! So tell us why you don't want big boobs."

"Do you remember me telling you about the boxer that my dad let live with us? Well, one day he said that he had an idea for some fun. He said that he knew a place at a construction entrance to Disneyland where we could sneak in and walk around. That sounded like an idea that Tony would have come up if he was alive. So I agreed to go.

"When we got to the Disneyland gate, he stopped the car and immediately started grabbing my boobs. He was being a jerk. I told him to leave me alone, or I would tell my dad. I told him that my dad would beat him up if he messed with me. I told him that my dad went to jail once, and he is not afraid to go back for beating up a punk. He started the car, and we left and drove home without another word being said. I hate it that guys wanna look at or grab my boobs. I hate having big boobs. I want little bitty boobs"

"Did your dad really go to jail," asked Cheryl.

"Yes," I replied. "I overheard my mom and granddad talking about it a long time ago. It had something to do with gambling. He wasn't violent. The only time he was violent was when he went to war. He said that he had to shoot men in the war. He was captured by the Japanese, and they tortured him. He has marks on his back where they beat him. One of his fingers is missing because they shot it off."

"Wow," all three girls said at once.

"Wait, I thought that you said your dad died in the war," questioned Cheryl.

"He did. My mom got married again when I was real little. That is why I have a different last name than my mom," I said sadly. "Anyway, I think that if my dad can live after being captured by the Japs, he can handle a punk boxer. I didn't tell my dad what happened. It really didn't matter because the boxer guy left not long after that."

"By the way, I think that we need to start shaving our legs and armpits. We are freshmen. We are old enough to start. We all have our periods now, don't we? My mom said that I can start shaving now," Brenda said proudly.

"I started last year," said Cheryl.

"Me too," I declared.

"Me too," Sandy laughingly said.

"None of the boys shave yet," Brenda said. "That's because they aren't as mature as us. Everyone knows that girls are more mature than boys."

"Are we going to the movies together this weekend?" I asked. "*Some Like It Hot* is playing. Marilyn Monroe is starring in it."

"Sounds good. Let's go," said Brenda.

Dear friend,

It would be fun to hear about your high school years. Were they your best years, worst years, or somewhere in between? Mine were somewhere in between. I loved hanging out with the church youth group, going to Youth for Christ Bible Club, working my first job at a television repair place, and getting a car. There were moments of embarrassment, insecurity, and identity struggles. There were also great friendships formed.

There were several of us who often sat under a tree at lunchtime and talked. Our conversations included talking about boys, the latest fashion or fad, teachers, and who likes who and why. It is with fondness that I recall our lunchtime conversations.

About the boob thing, I was very self-conscious about having boobs because I developed sooner than my friends, and I was bigger than my friends. To dress like, look like, and act like all the other girls was very important to me. I did not want to be *different* in any way.

I wish that I could have been confident about my appearance, like my current awesome friend, Ann-Marie. She is an amazing thirteen-year-old girl. Someone at school told her that her ears look like elf ears. She told the person that she is an elf, so that person better behave, or she will tell Santa Claus not to give her any toys for Christmas. Isn't that great! Some of Ann-Marie's friends believed that she truly was an elf, and they told her what they wanted for Christmas! Way to go, my dear confident Ann-Marie! She embraces her cute ears and is not ashamed of how God created her! She did not let the words of someone impact her in a negative way. Instead, she embraces who God created her to be! Ann-Marie is totally awesome.

So many times, we listen to the voices of others who try to tell us who we are.

Sometimes we tell ourselves lies about who we think that we are. You might be saying to yourself that you are not smart enough, pretty enough, good enough, or maybe even too much. I know that you do this. We all do.

I would like to recommend to you a wonderful book written by Steven Furtick, *Crash the Chatterbox: Hearing God's Voice Above*

All Others. That is it! That is what we need to do: hear, listen to, and believe the voice of God above all other voices, even our own voice that has whispered lies to us all our life.

Is it time to silence those negative thoughts about who you think you are and start believing the truth of who you are in Jesus? You are loved, you are beautifully and wonderfully made, you are precious to God, you are the apple of God's eye, and he rejoices over you. I need to repeat these things to myself daily.

May I make another suggestion? In your alone prayer time with God, ask him to reveal the truth that you need to hear most about who you are. Ask God to silence the negative voices in your head and magnify the voice of truth. What strengths, talents, and abilities has God gifted to you? Write them down.

I need to admit something to you. Sometimes I look in the mirror and see an old lady with wrinkles looking back at me. How can it be that I have wrinkles? In my mind, I am only forty-five or fifty years old, not a day older. Ha-ha-ha. I know that I was born in 1944, and that numbers don't lie. I am old. My age is a big number, but in my heart and mind, I don't think that I am a senior citizen.

I have found that replacing my negative view of myself with words of affirmation is a powerful, truth-telling experience. When I look in the mirror I say: I am beautifully and wonderfully made, I am the apple of God's eye, God is molding me into someone beautiful. I can do all things through Christ. I suggest that you take a minute and write down words of affirmation that God puts in your heart. Look in the mirror and joyfully declare those words for yourself.

I pray that you and I can embrace all of who we are, just as my dear friend Ann-Marie embraces her cute elf ears. Ann-Marie is beautifully and wonderfully made, and so are you. And me too.

In high school, I found an amazing club to join—Youth for Christ Bible Club. I also met and became best friends with Georgene. I hope that you enjoy reading about our adventures together at the Bible club.

Youth for Christ

"**Y**ou need to come to Youth for Christ with us," declared Delores. "It is fun, and the leader is so cute. We meet before school once a week. Come on. Go with us."

"Okay, okay, I'll go," I said.

The first day that I went, I met Georgene. We became best friends immediately. We saw each other every day at school and sometimes after school. We talked every day on the phone.

The club has officers, like president and treasurer. I don't much care about that, but Georgene wanted to be an officer. So she went to a Youth for Christ leadership conference where she met a really cute guy. She really liked him, and she thought that he liked her, but she was not sure. She decided that she needed a plan to get this cute guy to notice her. So we came up with a genius plan.

Every year, Youth for Christ has a huge graduation party at a fancy hotel. The Orange County and Long Beach Bible clubs come together for the gala event every year. There is a king and queen of the graduation party chosen by votes. Each vote costs a penny. So the Bible club that brings the most money knows their candidates for king and queen will be crowned king and queen of the graduation party. We have a small Bible club, so we knew that we needed to work hard to raise a lot of pennies to get our king and queen elected.

Georgene and I decided that if we could raise the most money and she was crowned the queen of the graduation party, surely this cute boy would be impressed with her and fall in love immediately.

Our goal—get the cute boy to notice Georgene. Our plan—make sure Georgene was the queen of the graduation party. All we had to do was make sure that we were the school that brought the most pennies to the graduation party. It was a piece of cake! We were ready to execute our plan! We knew that we could do it. Our club met, and we worked together to come up with the idea to have a fashion show.

The fashion show was amazing. Let me tell you about it. There was a cute boutique on Euclid Street called Merri's Feminine Fashions. The lady said that we could borrow as many clothes as we needed for our fashion show. We loved everything in her shop. She had a few cute dresses and a lot of skirts and sweaters. All the girls in our Youth for Christ Bible Club wanted to model the cute clothes.

I chose a dark blue skirt and white sweater with a blue silk scarf that I tied around my neck. I also modeled a really pretty dress that Mom bought me for the graduation party. It was a beautiful pink. It was full and flowing, so I bought two petticoats to wear under it. I felt like Cinderella in that dress! All I needed were glass slippers! A handsome prince would have been nice!

Priscilla's Cakebox provided lots of beautiful delicious cookies and Cal-Va Dairy provided punch. Georgene's mom let us use her fancy punch bowls. Someone went to the Dixie cup company, and they provided us with more cups than we needed. We also put out some peanuts and mints.

Someone told us that we could make even more money if we got stores downtown to advertise on a program that we could give to everyone who came. Peek Family Funeral Home provided a printed program and tickets. We even found a church that would let us use their fellowship hall.

We started selling tickets to kids at school and church. Everyone I talked to bought a ticket. Who knew this would be so easy! What fun it was to organize and get stuff together for the fashion show! We even gave our fashion show a name: Springtime Silhouettes.

The fashion show was a huge success. We sold a lot of tickets, so the fellowship hall was packed. Everyone loved the cookies and punch. Of course, the clothes were wonderful. What a great fashion show. We were proud of ourselves for pulling off such a huge fund-raising event.

I had a great idea for raising money at school. I bought a box of Tootsie Roll Pops for a really good price and sold them at school for twenty-five cents each. Practically all of the kids bought more than one pop. Most days I made ten dollars, and some days more. One day, a teacher put a stop to my money-making adventure. She told me that I had to stop selling candy because too many kids were eating their candy during their classes. Darn, that was easy money!

Georgene got a new dress at the fashion show so she could look great for the cute guy. Mike, the guy that we chose as the Garden Grove Club king also looked amazing. He had on a new suit. Our candidates for king and queen were amazing, and we confidently knew that they would get the most votes because we raised a lot of money.

The announcement finally came.

"The king and queen of the Tahitian Paradise 1962 graduation party are Mike and Georgene of Garden Grove High School!" the announcer proclaimed.

We were so excited! Georgene was the queen of the party! Perfect! We did it. Now she will surely be noticed by the cute guy.

Everyone did notice how great the Garden Grove High Youth for Christ king and queen looked. Probably the only one who did not notice was the cute guy. He was busy that night looking at his girlfriend whom he brought to the party. I wasn't sure whether to laugh or cry. To laugh seemed like the better option. Ha-ha-ha. You know the saying, "The best-laid plans…"

Dear friend,

So much for our great plan. You know the saying, "the best-laid plan…" Georgene had great plans to get noticed by a boy, but alas, he had eyes for someone else. The cool thing is that Georgene was not shaken at all. We had so much fun raising money, and the graduation party was amazing. Sure she was disappointed but not shaken. Everything about the party was perfect—the decorations, the good food, the music and, of course, a wonderful time hanging out with friends.

A couple of years later, that cute guy ended up marrying the girl who was his date for the graduation party. Later, Georgene married an amazing and wonderful man, Torben, from Denmark, who was completely devoted to her and their two boys. The cute guy and Georgene just weren't meant to be together. God had better plans for both of them.

It is so easy to decide what we want and then make big plans to get what we think that we need. Oftentimes we make plans and ask God to bless our plans rather than seek him and ask him what plans that he has for our life.

Let me tell you about the plan I had for myself. A few years ago, I decided that I wanted to find a cottage that I could rent. I am not crazy about apartments. I really, really like privacy. I kept thinking that I would love a little cottage, a cottage near a wooded area. Sounds great, right?

Looking in the newspaper, I found a rustic cottage on a river. It seemed so perfect. I had an appointment to go see the cottage when I got a call from the owner. He said that since we were expecting a hurricane, it might not be a good idea to come that day. He said that he was praying that the cottage would not flood. After the storm passed, he called again and said that he had good news. His cottage did not flood.

My reply was "Great, but I don't think your cottage is what I am looking for."

I found a pool house that seemed perfect. When I went to look at it, I saw that the pigs got out of the pen and were wandering in the yard. There was no kitchen and only a tiny heater for the entire pool house. It could have been a good fit, but I decided against the pool house. I told everyone I knew to be on the lookout for a cottage for me. I prayed and asked God for my cottage.

Three years later, as well as a move to Richmond, I was ready to give up on my cottage. My friend Amy suggested that I look on Craig's List. To my delight and surprise, there it was, my cottage. Well, it actually isn't a cottage. It is even better. I now live in a six-hundred-square foot dwelling attached to a stable where nine beautiful horses live. I hope you aren't laughing because I am serious. This place is perfect for me. It sits on a one-hundred-acre beautiful piece of land with woods and pastures. My only neighbor is my landlord, and I can't see his house from my windows or my stone patio. What more could I want?

It comes fully furnished with furniture that I love. The kitchen is perfect, with plenty of cabinets and counter space. Actually, my house is perfect for me. I have a stone patio, side yard where I planted flowers, and beautiful woods practically right outside my door. I think that it is better than a cottage!

I love having horses right outside my door. On weekends, I get to feed them and muck the stalls! I love it! I would never in a million years pray for a house connected to a barn. Nope, never.

The point of this story is that I prayed for years for a cottage. I expected him to give me a cottage where I was living, but that didn't happen. I did not expect to move to Richmond; however, it was all in God's plan. God's plan is so much better than the plan I had for myself. He has provided for me the perfect dwelling. It is in God's purpose and plan for me that I live in Richmond in a house attached to horse stables—my perfect dwelling.

Actually, in God is the perfect dwelling place. Psalm 90:9–10 says, "If you say, 'The Lord is my refuge,' and you make the Most High your dwelling, no harm will overtake you. No disaster will come near your tent."

God has a purpose for each of us. If you live many years, your purpose changes over time. God's purpose for me now is different than my purpose when I was a young wife and mother. There will never be a moment that God doesn't have a purpose and plan for us.

I attend the LifePoint Church. I would like to share with you a quote from the LifePoint website.

> God's vision for your life is to be fully alive. He wants you to know Him, find freedom, discover purpose, and make a difference. When we don't live out this vision, we can find ourselves feeling unfulfilled and lacking purpose.

By living out God's purpose for our life, we touch the lives of others and can become the catalyst for change and growth in the life of others.

My senior year was a difficult year at home. I didn't give much thought about God's vision for my life. I wasn't prepared for or ready for another *whoosh* in my life, but it came, anyway.

Whoosh

"Mom, put the knife down. Please, Mom! Don't do this." I cried.

"Listen to Rita. Put it down," demanded Dad.

"I can't take this anymore. I am leaving and going back to Kansas. We are going back to my house in Coffeyville," cried Mom.

"Please, Mom, please," I begged. She put down the knife and walked out of the room, sobbing.

I started feeling sick. *Not again!* My heart cried. I have vomited every day this week. When will it stop? I ran out the back door and started vomiting in the yard. My insides were piled up on the grass. My insides were churning; they had to come out. My hurt and pain had to come out. I couldn't hold my emotions in any longer. The roller-coaster ride of my mind and heart finally caught up with my physical body. All the anxiety and fear had nowhere to go but on the grass in my backyard.

Why does it have to be this way? I wondered to myself, *Why doesn't Dad get a regular job? Why is he always after a get-rich-quick plan? Why can't he just be like other dads and go to work and come home with a paycheck? Mom can't live like this, not knowing when we will not have a home, not knowing if someone will take our car in the middle of the night again. It seems like Mom is upset or angry all the time."*

It was just yesterday that my mom said to me, "I don't know who is dumber, you or John (my stepdad)."

What did I say? What did I do? Who knows? Who cares? Here we go again. I ran outside so as not to vomit on the floor. I didn't want anyone to know that I have been vomiting.

I prayed and called out to God to help my stomach calm down. I always feel better until I see Mom or Dad. I sometimes see my mom look at my dad with anger in her eyes. I sometimes see her look at me with anger in her eyes. I can't figure out what I am doing wrong. Maybe there is just something wrong with me. Maybe no one can love me. I don't know what is wrong with me. I think that my mom used to love me. Why did she stop?

Whoosh! Here it comes again. My insides always spill all over the floor or the grass. I hate it that this keeps happening.

When will this end? I feel like Mom when she says "I can't take this anymore." I feel better if I read or hang out with my friends. I need to leave. I am going away to college. There is a great college in Arkansas. That is my plan. I will go away to college and never come back.

Dear friend,

Sixty years ago! That is how long ago that I heard those painful words from my mom about being dumb and saw the anger in her eyes. Sixty years ago, I vomited in the yard or bathroom every single day until I left for college. It was sixty years ago, yet in some respects, it seems like only yesterday.

Let me tell you about my mother. She was a sweet, kind, caring woman. She would give whatever she had to anyone who was in need. She was quiet, but when she spoke, her words were worth listening to. I love my mother so much. She died of melanoma cancer in 2007.

As an adult, I am able to look back on that time in my mom's life and realize that she, too, was undoubtedly living in anxiety and fear. Her marriage was not healthy or happy. She spoke those hurtful words to me from a place of her own pain. I know that she never thought that I was dumb. However, those words became words of truth in my own heart and mind. That is exactly where Satan wants us—in a place of believing lies.

When I told Georgene about my plan to go to Arkansas, she said that was a bad idea. She told me about a better school much closer to home. She suggested that we check out Biola together. Georgene convinced me that I should stay in California and attend Biola with her.

When I left for college, I didn't leave behind my false belief of being dumb or my fear of others leaving me. In my heart, I felt abandoned by my dad, Tony, and Granddad. I didn't leave behind the memory of my mom saying that she didn't know who was dumber, me or my dad. Those words and fears of being left followed me to college.

Truthfully, my fears and false beliefs formed in childhood and teenage years have followed me in every relationship and situation for sixty years. I am probably safe in saying that every single one of us has false beliefs about ourselves as well as fears that have followed us around in our job, at home, and in our relationships.

My false beliefs and insecurities showed up one day when I was in a job interview for a teaching position. I met with the superintendent of a large school district near where I lived. The superintendent said to me that my letters of recommendation were amazing, and my college grades were perfect. He said that he was surprised that I didn't already have a great teaching job. He asked me why it was that I hadn't been hired yet. My old thoughts about something being wrong with me kicked in. Instead of a confident response I simply said "I don't know." I knew in that moment that I would not get the job. I believed a lie that I was dumb, and I allowed the lie to control my thoughts as well as my interview.

I could have told him that I was nervous and then taken a deep breath and confidently talked about my ability to see and help the "unseen" child as well as my patience with the slow learner. I could have told him that I have great skills in teaching children. I didn't do any of that. Instead, in that moment, I allowed myself to believe that I am dumb. I had not yet learned the skill of taking my thoughts captive. I had not learned that I have value and worth. In that moment, I was the insecure little girl believing a lie about myself.

My false beliefs about myself have impacted every single relationship in my life. In so many relationships, I have expected and waited for the time when a friend would stop loving me or realize that there is something wrong with me and then leave. I believed the lie that my mom stopped loving me. This has been my destructive false thinking: "Just because you love me today doesn't mean that you will love me tomorrow. I am dumb. There is something wrong with me."

It would be such a cool story to tell you that I am 100 percent free of believing the lies of Satan. It would be cool and awesome to tell you that in my close relationships, I am mature, wise, and never fear that I will be "left." Wouldn't it be great if I could tell you that I walk in victory every single day of my life?

Wait! Stop! I can walk in confidence! I can have the victory! I can believe and see truth, light, and love in my life!

Walking in victory demands that I see the negative beliefs about myself for what they are—*lies*—lies that Satan wants to use to destroy me. Walking in victory requires that I surrender every situation and person in my life to Jesus daily. This is not a set-it-andforget-it kind of deal. This is a constant take-control-of-my-thoughts and surrender-to Jesus kind of deal.

I have found that knowing who I am in Christ is healing and life changing. I am his child (Romans 8:14) and his beloved (Romans 9:5). He is the Lover of my soul (Psalm 23:3). I am the apple of God's eye (Zechariah 2:8). This would be a good time to put this book down for now and go get your Bible. Please find and read these verses in your Bible and then meditate on the truth that God speaks to your soul.

Hi, I am glad you are back.

I have also found that the affirmation and love from other Christians is also healing and life changing. We should encourage each other, speak words of truth to each other, and tell each other the truth of who we know each other to be in Christ. That is why I am writing this letter to you. You and I need to know that we are loved by Jesus. You and I need to believe that we can have victory through our faith in Jesus. We need to surrender those false beliefs that we have held on to far too long.

Your beautiful friend might need to know that you value her as a friend for who she is. That confident overachiever might need to know that he or she is valued as a person, not for what he or she does. I am an old lady with wrinkles. My heart and spirit is lifted when someone calls me beautiful. Tell others who they are. They need to hear it.

Trust me, we all need to hear that we are valued, wanted, and beautifully and wonderfully made.

Victory can be my story and your story as well. We can catch ourselves believing a lie from Satan, rebuke him, and speak the truth of God's word into our own hearts. We can enjoy loving, awesome, close relationships. What is cool and wonderful is that we can live life to the fullest. Jesus wants us to live life to the fullest.

> The thief comes only to steal and kill and
> destroy; I have come that they may have life, and
> have it to the full. (John 10:10)

We need Jesus every moment of every day. We need to allow our thoughts to go to Jesus and his incredible love for us. We do not need to allow the whoosh in our lives to control us. I know some things to do when I feel insecure, unloved, fearful, or doubtful. Let's look at some things that you and I can do.

First and foremost, we need to stay in the Word. Simple devotionals are great, but I need to open my Bible and study and ponder what I am reading and ask God to make it relevant to my day. I pray and seek Jesus during my morning time with him as well as throughout my day.

Worshipping through music encourages my soul and takes me from a place of negativity to a place of pure joy. I have a playlist that I listen to daily. In my car, I often listen to praise music as well. I gotta admit here that I do listen to other music as well. Ha-ha.

Reading books written by others who have struggled and found victory is very helpful for me to redirect my thinking. There are so many amazing Christian authors: Bob Goff, Steven Furtic, Stacie Eldridge, John Eldridge, Lysa TerKeurst, Joyce Meyer, Beth Moore, and Francis Chan are a few of my favorites.

Worshipping with others encourages me more than I can express. Listening to and applying what I hear from the pulpit helps me grow and mature in Christ. I take notes, ponder, and ask Jesus to help me apply the words spoken to my heart by my pastor, Daniel Floyd. He reminds us often that the evil one comes to steal, kill, and destroy, but Jesus comes so that we can live life to the fullest. I don't have to wait until I get to heaven to have a full, blessed life.

I attend a small group during the week. We love and pray for each other. We are in contact with each other daily through GroupMe, praying for and encouraging each other.

I also need and have relationships in my life that encourage me. I believe that we women need the fellowship, love, and encouragement of other women. I don't mean to get together and gossip or talk about our husbands or kids but to be the voice of love, godly wisdom, and support for each other.

We need to find and nurture relationships. I have a friend who pours truth, light, and love into my heart. She teaches me love. She gives me flowers! I sometimes get to share movie night with another friend. Sometimes I invite a friend for lunch or dinner. I have another friend who will often call and ask how I am doing. There are also friends in my life that I rarely see, but we share a closeness that encourages me in so many ways. Our common bond is Jesus.

You might be thinking, *I don't have friendships.* I get it. I am an introvert who fears being left. So I get the "no friend" thing. However, we need each other. I suggest that you get involved in your church, volunteer, join a small group. Pursue friendships. You will be glad you did.

I think that I have already told you that I tend to be a slow learner. Here I am at seventy-six, still learning how to walk with Jesus, surrender my thoughts to him, believe the truth of his Word, and know and believe every minute of every day that I am loved. I might not be the smartest chick in the world, but one thing I know is that I need Jesus every moment of every day.

Let me tell you about yesterday. I did all the right things. I read my Bible, prayed, listened to praise music while I exercised. I sent a text to a friend and then spent some time writing this book. Off to work I went.

When I got to work, it wasn't long before a coworker said something ugly to me. She probably was just having a bad day and didn't mean to sound ugly. Next, I didn't hear back from the friend that I texted. So I started thinking, *That was probably a stupid text anyway, and besides, my friend is too busy to text me. I bet I messed up, and now that coworker hates me. Why am I such a mess up?* On and on my thoughts continued. Before I even knew that it was happening, I was suddenly in a bad mood. At that moment, I caught myself and began to praise Jesus and surrender my thoughts to him.

The minute that I wake up, it helps me to begin my day with praise to Jesus in my heart. I praise him for who he is and the blessings that he showers on my life. I can choose to be awake and optimistic for a great day or wake up with a complaining heart of all that I have to do during my day. The next thing that I do is to start my playlist.

I don't know about you, but for me, taking my thoughts captive and walking in love requires me to be spiritually awake and alert all day every day. It also requires listening to the voice of God in my heart. Sometimes it requires me doing stuff I would rather not do, like being nice and loving toward a coworker or rude person that I might encounter. I would rather ignore the coworker, but Jesus would rather that I love, live, walk, and act in an attitude of love and joy. Some days I fail miserably, others I do okay, and then there are days that I walk in peace and joy.

Do you like movies? I love going to the movie theater to watch a movie. Join me and my college friend in Hollywood where we went to see *How the West Was Won.*

How the West Was Won

"We gotta go see *How the West was Won*," I declared to Carol. "The cast is amazing. Debbie Reynolds, John Wayne, Gregory Peck, James Stewart, and Henry Fonda are starring in it and a bunch of other big-time stars. I heard that the music is amazing."

"I think we should go see it in Hollywood," Carol said excitedly.

"Yes, definitely Hollywood," I agreed.

We went to Hollywood to the most beautiful theater that I had ever seen! I felt like we were in a palace or a beautiful church. I have been to many movie theaters, but this one was beyond what I had ever experienced. The high ceilings were breathtakingly beautiful. To me, they looked like the ceilings that could be in European cathedrals, not that I have ever been to Europe. Even the bathroom was amazing. It would be perfect for a king, decorated with a fancy marble counter, ornate mirror, and fancy soap and hand lotion. The hand towels were like a thick paper towel but very nice. Everywhere I looked, I saw beauty.

After walking around like country bumpkins, being amazed at everything, we got popcorn, candy, and sodas at the concessions counter in the carpeted lobby and sat down and excitedly waited for the movie to begin. It sorta' felt like this was my first movie experience. I have been to many movies, but never in Hollywood!

"The best three hours of my life—amazing songs, beautiful stars, wonderful story, and the perfect theater. I don't want the evening to end," I declared.

We went outside and immediately linked arms and skipped down the street, singing as loudly as we could the Debbie Reynolds song, "Raise a Ruckus."

> Come along little children, come along
> While the moon is shining bright
> Now get on board going down the river float
> We gonna raise a ruckus tonight.

We laughed and sang, enjoying the afterglow of a fun evening at the movies. We saw a small coffee shop and decided to top off our wonderful evening with coffee and tea. We continued our fun movie experience by talking about the cast as though we were big-time movie critics or gossip-column writers.

"I can't believe that Eddie Fisher," I declared. "He is such a jerk. Why would he leave Debbie Reynolds for another woman? I know Elizabeth Taylor is beautiful, but Debbie, Eddie, Todd, and Carrie Fisher were such a beautiful little family. Eddie and Debbie were the perfect Hollywood couple"

"I think that affairs and divorce are a part of the Hollywood culture," exclaimed Carol.

"You are right," I agreed.

Monday morning, Carol and I were in for a big surprise.

"Did you read the daily bulletin?" I asked Carol.

"Yes, I did," she replied. "Can you believe it? The bulletin said that *How the West Was Won* is not an educational or historical movie. They told us that we cannot go see it! I know that we agreed to live by and follow the rules when we came to college here, but some movies are okay to see. I don't like the rule that we cannot go to movies. We should be allowed to go to movies." Carol was already shouting.

"Keep it down," I warned. "I don't need any more trouble. I have already had to go see the dean of women twice."

"Really?" asked Carol.

"Yeah, once, I came in after curfew, and I was not repentant, so I had to go see the dean. Then one time, I wore pants outside of the dorm. Georgene and I were going somewhere, and we decided to wear pants. Georgene isn't a rule-breaker kind of person. So if she thought it was okay to wear pants that day, then I was okay with it. It didn't seem like a big deal to us. Evidently someone thought that it was a big deal because we got called in to talk to the dean.

"When I got sent to the dean the second time, she asked me to think about what Paul would do before I do something. Really! Who knows what Paul would do! I'm sure that he liked to have fun once in a while. I know that Paul spent most of his time sharing the gospel and writing letters to the churches. I want to tell kids about Jesus and work in a local church and teach all the time," I explained.

"Did you tell her that?" asked Carol.

"No, all I said was 'Yes, Ma'am.' I think that is all she wanted to hear. I gotta stay out of trouble. As long as I tell her what she wants to hear, everything will be okay. I gotta keep everything good because I am already on academic probation. Chemistry is killing me."

Dear friend,

I enjoyed so many new and exciting experiences in my two years at Biola. I was living away from home, I met so many amazing people, and I loved learning. However, there were challenges for me as well. There were so many rules to follow, most of which didn't make sense to me. I struggled with both following rules and studying. At this particular time in my life, I didn't see the "prize" or result of studying or following rules.

One of the rules was that we were to be in our rooms at 8:00 p.m., studying. Since I didn't have good study skills and preferred to hang out with friends in my dorm, that rule was sometimes ignored. When I was caught breaking a rule, I was pretty good at talking my way out of trouble. Going to the dean of women truly didn't bother me a whole lot. I just told her what I knew she wanted to hear. I was very good at reading adults and usually knew what they wanted to hear.

Have you ever seen the TV show *Leave It to Beaver*? It was a sitcom in the '50s and '60s. It is the story of a wholesome family where the boys, Wally and Theodore (Beaver), learn life lessons each episode. In the show, there was a character named Eddie Haskell. He always spoke politely to teachers and parents. Eddie knew just the right thing to say to adults. He was a "Yes, sir; yes, ma'am" kind of guy. On the surface, he appeared to be a perfect kid who followed all the rules. However, in his dealings with other kids, quite the opposite was true. It turns out that he would sometimes lie to adults and bully Beaver.

His heart was not in the "right place." Here is a quote from Eddie to give you an idea of what I am talking about: "Wally, if your dumb brother tags along, I'm gonna—oh, good afternoon, Mrs. Cleaver. I was just telling Wally how pleasant it would be for Theodore to accompany us to a movie." The thing with Eddie is that he knew the "language" of adults. The same way that I knew what the dean wanted to hear, Eddie knew what Beaver's mom and other adults wanted to hear.

We sometimes say to others what we know they want to hear. We Christians know the "right things" to say and do when talking to other Christians. We know the "language." "God's got this" or "God is in control" we might say without thinking about what that truly means. We might declare "God is good" but truly only believe it when things are going our way. "I will pray for you" we say and then forget to pray until we see that person again. We know the right times to hoot and holler at a church service, the right times to clap or get excited.

We know the "rules." It is possible to leave church knowing we have said and done all the right things. *All is good*, we may be thinking. *I've done what I need to do this week to please God and other Christians*. Then we leave church and talk about others, do our own thing, and live a life that is not honoring to God.

Please do not misunderstand me. I truly know that God does have me at all times because he is in control. What the pastor is saying deserves a clap and maybe even a hoot and holler. I know that God is good, even when trials and pain come my way. He is good and faithful to be with me through it all.

However, I also know that it can be easy for us to repeat the "Christian language" so much to each other so that it becomes a shallow response to someone experiencing deep pain and struggles. If I speak words of encouragement from my head, trying to tell someone what they want to hear rather than from a heart of love, of what value are the words?

When I hear a truth spoken from the pastor, I might clap and get excited. I love hearing truth spoken. What is important is that I remember my *church* excitement on Monday. I want to remember that same truth when being attacked by lies from Satan and then clap in my heart and get excited and hoot and holler because I know the truth that I am loved, that God has me, that I am His, and I can proclaim, "Great are you, Lord and love of my life!" The Sunday excitement is good; however, the Monday excitement is even better.

A teacher of the law was listening to Jesus. Surely the teacher knew the commandments as well as the right things to say. He knew the "language." I assume that he followed the commandments. He asked Jesus which of the commandments was the most important. That is a good question. Of all the rules that we are supposed to follow, what is the most important of all? Jesus replied,

> Love the Lord your God with all your heart and with all your soul and with all your mind with all your strength. The second is this, love your neighbor as yourself. There is no commandment greater than these. (Mark 12:30–31 NIV)

Simply stated, "Love God, love people." It is simple yet so profound.

Do you remember me telling you about my friend Darryl? He is the one who believes that God created a beautiful blade of grass just for him. Darryl and his wife, Gloria, live out Mark 12:30–31 in their lives. Darryl has as his license plate LGLP. If you meet Darryl, it won't be long before love God, love people comes up in conversation.

Gloria is not the outgoing talker like Darryl. She loves her family and friends with the love of Jesus. She has a generous heart and treats others like family. If you need a place to stay, she has a spare bedroom waiting for you.

When someone shares with us their struggle, it is so easy to say the familiar words that we so often say to each other. However, perhaps no words at all need to be spoken. Maybe a hug is what is needed. When someone's life is falling apart, maybe they need the freedom to talk, be heard, seen, and loved. When someone's life is falling apart, they don't need shallow words spoken from the head. What heals, soothes, and brings peace are words of love from Jesus spoken from the heart. I pray that Jesus will give me the strength, wisdom, and love to not be a people pleaser like Eddie Haskell but, rather, to be the voice and heart of the love of Jesus.

I am a little concerned here that what I am saying might be misunderstood. What I want to say is that we need to listen to the one who is hurting, listen to Jesus and ask him how we should respond. When we do respond, we need to be careful not to use the sometimes *shallow* words that can become an empty "Christian speak" rather than the voice of Jesus.

Everyone has an opinion, ideas, and a belief system. I heard so many voices in the '60s. What is one to believe? I would like to share with you the many voices that I heard in college.

Voices

Wow, this is crazy. I didn't realize that so many people have ideas and beliefs that are different from mine. I think that maybe I was sheltered and told what to believe as a teenager. At California Baptist College, I am learning that so many people have different ideas that describe their truth. I sorta' liked it better when I was told what to believe. Now I have to make up my own mind what is truth and what is not truth. I wish that someone could help me decide what to believe. What am I to believe?

Here are some of them:

> A well-meaning friend who wants me to succeed:
> "Surely you know that you will never get a job at a church. Have you ever heard of a woman Christian education director or associate pastor? No, you haven't. So why are you a Christian education major? You should change your major and change your goals. Do it now, before it is too late."

> A friend pondering whether to choose the path of being a missionary:
> "A missionary. That is what I want to be. Of course, it will be a hard life, but I can do it. Me and my future husband will probably go to Africa. That is where the true dedicated missionaries go. The only hard part is that you have to

raise your own financial support. Not everyone can do that. I guess you have to be good at talking to church people, begging for money. Hmmm, maybe being a missionary isn't a good idea. What do you think, Rita? Do you think that God could be calling me to be a missionary?"

My roommate:

"I know a school that you should check out. They have a great sociology department. You would love it there. They are not so crazy strict like it is here. Check it out. It is California Baptist College."

A college professor:

"Woman was created to be the helpmate of man. There is no greater honor than being a pastor's wife. You can be the best pastor's wife by supporting your husband in every way. Since a young girl doesn't know if she will end up being a pastor's wife, she should be prepared by going to college, just in case God calls her to be a pastor's wife.

"Young girls should learn to play the piano so she can play at the church where her husband serves. She should also learn to be an excellent cook so she can provide meals for the church family.

"A woman best serves God as she serves her husband as he serves the church. However, a good college education and teaching credentials gives a young woman something to fall back on if something happens to her husband, and she needs to support herself or her husband."

A dear friend:

"Have you read *The Feminine Mystic*, written by Betty Friedan? Finally, someone wrote a book about what I already know to be true. Women are not meant to be little sissies controlled by men. My mom is so unhappy. She doesn't get to do what she really enjoys. Actually, I doubt that she knows what she truly enjoys. I believe that she was taught that happiness is found in the role of spouse, mother, and housewife. If she didn't have us, she would probably think that she is not needed in life and would be depressed.

"I am not going to live like my mother. I am going to pursue self-fulfillment through my education. My life will not consist of finding a man, getting married, and having babies. I was created for more than this. I will pursue my dreams and my desires."

A college professor:

"I don't get why there is an issue here. A fetus is not a baby. When a woman gets pregnant, a seven-pound baby does not instantly appear in her belly. Before life happens, the sperm fertilizes the egg and forms a fetus the size of a tadpole. A fetus is not a baby.

"When a woman knows that she is not ready to be a mother, she should be allowed to remove the fetus from her own body. She is aborting the potential for life but not life. Being truly human happens only when one life interacts with another life."

A family member:

"You need to understand that the soldiers in Vietnam are baby killers. Our soldiers are killing innocent people. They are not fighting to keep America safe. They are fighting a war that does not need to be fought. We need to get out of Vietnam now. Our military men are nothing but cowards. They need to stand up and say that they will not fight an unnecessary war against innocent people. We should be making love, not war.

A politician:

"We need to contain communism. It is everyone's job to stop the threat of communism. Our men are keeping us free from the threat of communist rule in the United States."

A challenger to containment:

"Why not victory? Victory in Vietnam is what we should expect. We need victory now. We need to send more troops now."

A dear friend:

"We need to fight the establishment. We need to fight against war. We need to have our voices heard."

A man I was very close to:

"We need to get married. If we get married, I will not have to go to Vietnam. Please marry me."

A professor:

"It just makes sense. There is so much scientific evidence to prove the big bang theory. The elements in our bodies include oxygen, carbon, iron, and nickel. Those same elements are actually stardust. Stardust is in us. That same stardust is as old as the universe."

Dear friend,

There are so many thoughts and so many beliefs. Each of us has our own personal childhood and life experiences as well as voices we heard from people that we respect. Those experiences and voices have shaped who we are and what we believe.

Today is no different from the '60s in that our belief system is constantly being challenged. This could be a time of confusion or a time to stand on what we know to be true from the Word of God as well as what he speaks into our heart and lives.

God has created each of us with our own talents, spiritual gifts, and abilities. He formed us in our mother's womb to be the individuals he needs us to be to fulfill our purpose. We are unique. We are not carbon copies of each other. We should not expect every other person to think like, act like, or be like the person God created us to be.

When I was in high school, Georgene's mom found out that my family were Democrats. My dad was in a union for plumbers and pipe fitters. As a union man, he believed that only Democrats wanted to fight for the little guy and unions. My dad always said that the Republican Party was the party of big business.

One day, Georgene's mom said to me that I could not possibly be a Democrat and a Christian at the same time. When she found out that I went to the movies as well as being from a family of Democrats, she was convinced that I was a sinner, headed straight for hell. There was no hope for me! However, that did not stop her from loving me and having me over for dinner. She was not trying to be judgmental; she was simply acting on what she believed to be true: Democrats can't possibly be Christians.

Why is it that we sometimes demonize those who hold different beliefs from ours? You might agree with the views held by Georgene's mom that Democrats can't possibly be Christians. Here is a little-known fact: Billy Graham at one time was a registered Democrat. I sometimes had to tell people that to get them to back off from trying to "bring me to Jesus." Ha-ha-ha. Billy Graham became a Republican during the presidency of Richard Nixon. Billy Graham had meaningful relationships with both political parties.

It is okay to hold different views from those of your friend or colleagues. We do not need to be carbon copies of each other. My friend Birt told me a cool story about square watermelons. Yes, there is such a thing as square watermelons.

Square watermelons are grown in Japan as ornamental fruit. Each individual small melon is placed in a box in the field. As the melon grows, it conforms to the shape of the box that it has been placed in. That's right, it grows into the shape of a cube. When it is time, the square watermelon is taken from the box, and a beautiful ribbon is placed on top, ready to be sent to market. The melons can sell for as much as one hundred dollars. The watermelon cube is actually beautiful, with perfect vertical stripes and perfect shape.

However, since the watermelon does not fully ripen in the box, its contents are useless. The watermelon cannot be eaten and enjoyed as a tasty fruit. To be enjoyed as a sweet fruit, the watermelon needs space to grow and mature. The melon has value, but not for its contents since it cannot be eaten. What we do have is a beautiful watermelon cube. The watermelon cubes stack beautifully on top of each other and make a beautiful display at the market. Each melon is the exact size as all the other melons. However, they are useless as a tasty fruit.

We, too, need space as well as a personal relationship with Jesus to grow and mature to become the person that he created us to be, not carbon copies of each other but beautiful individuals. As we grow and mature in Christ, we have tasty morsels of truth, light, and love to share with others.

We can and should celebrate our individuality. God created each of us with talents, abilities, and spiritual gifts. However, we should not expect everyone to be exactly like the person God created us to be.

We obviously are going to disagree. Our political beliefs could be different from that of an acquaintance, coworker, or even family member. That is understandable and normal. However, to demonize and hate those who disagree with our view is not acceptable and should not be normal behavior. I never in my lifetime have seen so much negative rhetoric of hate and judgment coming from public figures.

To find truth, we should always look to the Word of God. It says in 2 Timothy 3:16, "All scripture is inspired by God and profitable for teaching, for reproof, for correction, for training in righteousness."

I believe that it is wise to seek godly counsel when issues arise in which we are uncertain about what God's word says about a particular issue. I also believe that we should listen to the voices in our lives that speak godly truth and wisdom when the truth needs to be spoken.

I gotta say here that another voice I have learned to listen to is the voice of a child. I am sure that you have heard the idiom "Out of the mouths of babes." It comes from Psalms 8:2, "Out of the mouth of babes and sucklings hast thou ordained strength."

I know from experience, as do you, that out of the mouth of babes can often come great wisdom. My friend Adalynne is such a wise kid. I remember one time we were driving in my car, and I was angry about something really dumb. I was going on and on about something silly. I recall Adalynne saying, "I know that I am just a kid, but I need to say something to you." Then she began speaking truth, light, and love into my life. She spoke wisdom from a place of love and wisdom from God. Truth was spoken to my heart that day. I truly believe that we—parents, teachers, and leaders—would do well to listen to the voices of children more than we do. From the voice of a child, we might just hear truth, light, and love.

My next story takes us to a wedding. Who doesn't love a wedding? Come with me to see what story unfolds at the wedding of my college roommate.

Is This Love?

O ne of my best friends is my roommate, Roberta. She is funny, really smart, and one of the most interesting people that I had ever met. She seems to know a little bit about everything—social correctness, politics, education, and all the current hot topics. She stays on top of what is going on. Roberta is such an awesome person! When she asked me to be in her wedding, I was really excited. I would have been even more excited had I known that I would meet my future husband at her wedding! Let me tell you the story.

One day, while Roberta and I were sitting in our dorm room talking about her upcoming wedding, Roberta said that she needed to go home to get something that she needed in planning her wedding. I had a car, so I drove her to her parent's house, which wasn't far away. She said that she would just run into the house and grab what she needed and run back out. So I waited in the car.

She is taking too long, I thought to myself.

Just about the time that I was ready to get out of the car, a tall muscular guy walked up to the car, looked inside, and said, "Hi, sis!"

I turned my head and saw him smiling at me.

When he realized that I wasn't "sis," he laughed and said, "Oh, sorry. I thought you were my sister sitting there."

I shyly replied, "Hi, I'm Rita. Roberta and I go to Biota together."

With that smile still on his face, he said "Hi, nice to meet you" and went into the house.

What! One sentence, that's all he has to say. "Nice to meet you." Not much of a talker, I thought to myself.

When Roberta came out, she said, "I think my brother likes you. He said that you are cute. He came all the way from Virginia just to be in my wedding. He is stationed at an army post in Virginia."

"Seems nice," I said. I wasn't much of a talker either. Ha-ha.

At the wedding, Ed and I had a few opportunities to talk. He was so easy and comfortable to talk to. He asked me if I wanted to go on a picnic with him. Of course, I said yes. I love picnics. Going on a picnic with a guy who looks great in an army uniform sounded like a good idea.

Just like Roberta, Ed seemed to know a little bit about everything too. It turns out that he was a talker! Good thing because I wasn't. He did enough talking for the both of us. He was funny too. At least, I thought so.

At one point, when we were sitting under a tree, he leaned in and kissed me. He didn't awkwardly grope me or drown me in a slobbery kiss. It was nice, maybe even perfect.

We went on a few dates, then Ed asked me to marry him. He was the nicest, sweetest guy that I had ever met. He treated me so well, but I couldn't marry him. I was still in college. I didn't know what I wanted to do with my life, and he was in the military living in Virginia. And there was Vietnam. He could be sent to Vietnam at any time.

Ed went back to Virginia and, later, was deployed to Vietnam. We wrote letters, and I thought about him often. I wanted things to work out for us, but I just didn't see how they could.

In the meantime, due to poor study skills and poor decisions, I was academically dismissed from Biola. I was determined to get a college degree. Someone told me that I should check out California Baptist College. I was told that if I was able to bring up my GPA by taking classes in the summer, then I could enroll in the fall as a regular student, not a student on probation. With a lot of determination and hard work, I made all As in summer school and was able to continue at CBC. In the fall, I enrolled in classes as a sociology major.

After I graduated from California Baptist College, I decided that I did not want to pursue a career in social work. I found a job at a small Christian school. I thought about Ed often. I missed him so much. After exchanging a few more letters, I decided to move to Virginia to start a new life with an awesome, sweet, kind man whom I loved.

We were married in Ohio, where my parents were temporarily living. My mom made my dress and cake as well as dresses for Raelene and Karen. Raelene and Karen were my bridesmaids.

Wait a minute! I have not told you about Karen. Karen is my sister. She was born my freshman year in college. When she was a baby, I was convinced that she was the smartest little person that God had ever created. I expected her to start reading books when she was a year old. No kid was smarter than my sister Karen.

Anyway, back to the wedding. Everything was so beautiful. My mom was so amazingly talented. She took Wilton cake decorating classes and made cakes for special occasions for our family as well as friends. Even though the wedding was very small, my mom made it awesome and beautiful with her artistic abilities.

We could not afford a honeymoon, so after the wedding, we left for Virginia to start our new life together—together in love.

Dear friend,

What is love? Is it a romantic experience, butterflies in your stomach, living happily ever after, riding off in the sunset with the love of your life, or maybe just a warm puppy? We as young girls, and women sometimes, dream about one day finding that one true love, the one to whom we will give of ourselves.

As a woman, I love those stories of finding *true love*. So many books and movies depict the fun as well as tragedy found in finding our true love. Nicolas Sparks's romantic drama novels are so great! His books show us the beauty in finding our true love as well as heartbreak in finding our true love. His stories are always beautiful and sometimes tragic.

Romantic comedies are so much fun to watch. First, the guy and the girl hate each other. Then all of a sudden, they fall in love! Isn't love, the dream of true love, and stories of love fun?

I love it when there is a twist in finding true love. In the movie *Maleficent*, the kiss of her true love that awakened Aurora from eternal sleep was the kiss of her godmother. No truer love was that of Maleficent for Aurora, as unlikely as it seemed.

What I have realized in the past few years is that love is a choice. I have heard it said that you can't choose who you fall in love with. Maybe not, but sustaining true from the soul love is a choice we make every single day. It is worth saying one more time: love is a choice.

In marriage, friendships, or in our workplace relationships, we choose whether or not we will love. Love is a choice. So often we want to define love by whether or not we are experiencing a warm, fuzzy feeling. In reality, we choose to live love. We choose whether or not to forgive, whether or not to be patient, kind, forgiving, angry or not angry. For the complete list of what love "is" read 1 Corinthians 13. These verses tell us how to live out our love for others in marriage, friendships, and those we meet along the way. I pray that you and I will choose love today and every day. Choose love, my dear friend.

In my past, I did not make the choice to choose love. In my brokenness, I was not following the path of love. I chose my own way. My husband and I were together yet apart.

Together, yet Always Apart

"Are you really coming back to California?" asked Sue excitedly. "I am so excited! Devona is here. Her husband is in Vietnam too. You guys should be roommates! Really you should!"

Ed was deployed to Vietnam again. Rather than stay in Virginia by myself, we decided that I should go to California the year that he would be away. My family was living in Ohio but told me that they would be moving back to California soon. So I decided to find a place to live in California.

I called my friend Sue and told her that I was coming to California. I met Sue while I was in college. My roommate came to play the piano at the church where Sue's dad was the pastor. I came with my roommate to Sue's church. Sue and I became instant friends. She was so much fun, and she and I had great conversations. We shared an instant connection. I enjoyed being with her so much.

Sue's dad, Pastor Norris, saw that I needed connection with a family while away at college. His family became family to me in so many ways.

The Sunday that I came to church after being away, friendships and love were renewed with Sue's parents, Norris and Ruby, and siblings, Craig and Sonia. Now Devona and Gina would become part of my life. My first Sunday back, Sue stood before the church and declared that she was grateful for my return to California and grateful that we were able to pick up as though I had never left. I was thinking to myself, *Wow! Sue is grateful for me. I have never heard anyone say that they were grateful for me.*

Ed and I wrote letters while he was in Vietnam. He came home briefly when his dad died. We obviously were together as a married couple, yet there was an emotional distance. My husband was distant in miles, and I remained distant emotionally. I was living from a wounded place in my heart.

When Ed returned to the States, I was happy to see him. When he returned, the US Army sent us to Texas briefly, then back to Virginia.

We were together at last, yet there still existed in my heart and soul wounded places that kept us apart. I was not emotionally connected to Ed and was not the supportive wife he needed. There were times that it seemed that we were two strangers living together. The wounded places in my heart kept me from connecting deeply with my husband.

Dear friend,

Truthfully, I am in no position, nor have any desire, to give out marital advice. What I can say is that I urge you to find and dwell in that place of intimacy with God. He does want our faith in him. I'm sure that he delights in our obedience and service. But more than anything, he desires union and intimacy with us. God desires to be the center of our universe, as well as the center of all marriages.

Are there wounded places in your heart and soul that keep you from connecting with others? The sad thing is that I didn't even think about or acknowledge my wounded places. I did a good job of burying any past hurts and wounds. They were buried so deeply that only God could do the excavating work of revealing and healing my wounded places.

Once my wounds were buried, I did a really *good* job at putting up an invisible wall around my heart. It was a wall so invisible that I wasn't aware of its existence. I kept myself "protected" and distant from intimacy with my husband. That was such a tragic mistake.

What I have found to be true is that intimacy with God was what I needed to tear down the wall that I had constructed my entire life. God used a trusted friend, who saw and knew that I was living behind a protective wall. Once my walls of protection were torn down, God's healing presence and love began to transform my life.

I wonder if it is true that all of us build walls around our hearts. Those walls are meant for protection but will ultimately keep connection, trust, and love from entering our heart. If the wall is big enough or thick enough, it can also keep us from true connection, trust, and love from God. God desires intimacy with us, not a superficial Sunday experience but true, from-the-heart intimacy. That intimacy can only happen if we allow God to guide us as we tear down that wall.

I believe that the process of tearing down the wall will be different with every single person. When we fall in love with Jesus and make him the center of our universe, he will begin the process of tearing down that wall.

Is God the center of your universe? As a young wife and mom, I was blessed to meet someone who knew Jesus as the center of her universe. I hope that you enjoy the story of my friend Leotia.

The Center of the Universe

There was a knock at my door. I didn't get visitors often, so I was excited when I heard the knock. I excitedly opened the door and, there to my surprise, was my friend from church, Leotia. I didn't know Leotia well, but from what I could tell, she was not like any person I had ever met.

She wore what looked to me like white hospital shoes. Comfort obviously mattered more to her than fashion. Speaking of fashion, Leotia wore polyester pants with an elastic waist band. Again, it was all about comfort. Most importantly, she always wore a smile, not just any smile but a smile that stated very clearly "Jesus loves you just exactly the way you are, and so do I." Just in case someone wasn't good at reading body language and smiles, she would be sure to tell them that Jesus loves them. I was delighted that Leotia had come to see me.

After talking small talk for a while, she asked me how I was doing. She said that she didn't see me at church Sunday and just wanted to check to make sure my family and I were doing well. Back in those days, we didn't have Facebook accounts where we could post our every move. We did have phones; however, personal face-to-face visits between friends happened often. We could stay in touch with each other's lives either at the many church events throughout the week or simply stop by the house of a friend to check up on them and see how they were doing. I miss those days of face-to-face visits.

I was glad Leotia checked on us this particular day. I was feeling grateful for my family but also acutely aware of the fragileness of life. My daughter Lori had been sick, and for some reason that day, I was worried that she could get sick again. Or maybe my other daughter, Kristy, could get sick. My thoughts seemed to be getting out of control when Jesus sent my friend Leotia to my door.

My daughter Lori was recovering from spinal meningitis. She was six months old, and my other daughter, Kristy, had just turned four. One day, Lori was completely listless and was running a fever. I decided to be on the safe side and took her to the doctor. After a very traumatic and painful spinal tap, the doctor declared that Lori had spinal meningitis. He said that she needed to be hospitalized immediately, with a nurse assigned to her for twenty-four-hour care. He said that the disease could cause brain damage, which could cause death or mental retardation.

I immediately called a couple of church friends and my family in California. My dad asked me if I had called the Pat Robertson prayer team. I had not, so he called them for me. We appreciated and wanted all the prayers that we could get.

A few days later, Lori was completely back to normal, laughing and playing. Much to the surprise and delight of her doctor, there was no brain damage. We were so excited to take her home. We praise Jesus that today, Lori is very gifted intellectually. She has a fine mind. All praise and glory goes to our Healer, Jesus Christ.

Anyway, back to my friend Leotia. I was delighted that she came visiting that day. That was the beginning of a long blessed relationship. She was sixteen years older than me and became a grandma to my girls, Lori and Kristy. Leotia and her husband, Bill, invited us to their home often for dinner and to play games.

Bill would grill ribeye steaks to perfection or slow cook a pot of pinto beans. After dinner, more often than not, Lori would announce that she was bored. That would be Leotia's cue to get out Rummikube, our favorite game to play. So Leotia, my girls, and I would play Rummikube. We had our own special way of playing. After one person "went out," we continued to play until everyone was out of tiles. There was never a true winner or loser, just players having fun and laughing.

Like so many precious women, Leotia experienced an incredibly difficult childhood.

She was often beaten by her mom and then locked in a closet. She was severely malnourished and near death when she was rescued by an elderly couple. They took her into their home as well as their hearts. The couple took Leotia to church where she was introduced to the Rescuer of her soul, Jesus. Jesus became her Lord and Savior.

What amazes me about her story is that she forgave her mother and the man who lived with them. She said that she loved them. I was also amazed at her love for Jesus. I had never met anyone who loved Jesus more or who knew and felt the love of Jesus more than my friend Leotia. I guess you could call her a Jesus freak.

Whenever we were in a public place together, she always managed to engage others in conversation. To engage in conversation with Leotia meant that she would tell you how loved you are by Jesus. She always asked every person she met if they knew her Jesus.

Of course, she would talk to others about Jesus. It makes sense because he was the center of her universe.

Sounds good, right? There were times that people were rude to her. There were times that I asked her to "tone down the Jesus talk." Unfazed by *criticism*, Leotia never missed an opportunity to share Jesus with others. He was the center of her universe. By her actions, she encouraged me to make Jesus the center of my universe as well. She chose to honor Jesus in words as well as action.

One day, around ten years into our friendship, Leotia and I were enjoying conversation, tea, and time together. Leotia said that she had something to tell me. She said that there were some church ladies who were gossiping about me and speculating about why my husband and I were getting a divorce. She told them that they should tend to their own business and their relationship with Jesus rather than criticize others who were hurting. She did not share with me the names of the ladies who were talking. She said to reveal names would just cause more hurt.

Leotia said that Jesus spoke to her heart through the conversation with those ladies to reveal to her that idle gossip is often disguised as a "concern" or a prayer request. The conversation or gossip sometimes starts when someone says, "We need to pray for..." or "I love her, but..." or "I would say the same thing to her if she was here." Someone can cover it up and make it look pretty by disguising gossip as love or a prayer request, but gossip is still gossip.

That particular conversation started as a prayer request to pray for me as I was in the midst of getting a divorce and ended in hurtful gossip. Leotia said that Jesus spoke to her heart to stop the gossip and to never be a part of such talk.

Leotia and Bill died of unrelated health issues on the same day in 2002. Can you imagine arriving in heaven to meet Jesus together? They were so blessed.

I miss my friend Leotia. I often wish that we could share one more game of Rummikube together or go visiting one more time with the intent of sharing the love of Jesus. Leotia and I sometimes went door-to-door inviting people to the trailer park mission chapel where we attended. Jesus was the center of Leotia's universe. She wanted everyone to know and experience the love of Jesus and allow him to become the center of their universe as well.

I wish that you could have met my friend Leotia. I bet that you would have loved her as much as I did—weirdness and all!

Dear friend,

I live and work in Ashland, Virginia. We call our town the Center of the Universe. I work at the Center of the Universe Chick-fil-A. What a joy and privilege to have the opportunity to serve others with love. I have the opportunity to make a difference in the lives of our guests by sharing a smile, great service, a kind word spoken, and a beautifully clean dining environment! I love our mission statement: "To be a restaurant of excellence, positively impacting our community and the world." How cool is that!

Living and working in the Center of the Universe reminds me daily to make Jesus the center of my universe. Truthfully, Jesus is teaching me daily what it means to make him the center of my universe.

Jesus was the center of Leotia's universe because of her love for him. When we fall in love with Jesus, he then becomes the center of our universe. At the beginning of my relationship with Jesus, I fell in love with reading my Bible, going to church, attending Bible studies, teaching children as well as serving at and attending church social events. I loved all that stuff. I probably loved the church life more than Jesus. My church life was the center of my universe.

I will later share with you my story of falling in love with Jesus. I fell in love with Jesus in a church environment, singing a worship song. I am excited to share that story with you. It is coming; I promise.

Bible teaching and preaching, Bible studies, and socializing together all play a vital role in our growth and maturity as Christians. We need preaching and teaching. We need each other. We need Christian social events. However, those practices and activities were never meant to take the place of our personal intimate relationship with God. Prayer is the place of intimate relationship.

There are many, many, many books written about prayer and how to pray. I have no desire to write another book about prayer. However, what I can write about is my very personal life experience. What I noticed in my prayer life was that the times that I spent the most time in prayer were the times that I was experiencing fear, conflict, or pain.

Those were the times that I sought God the most. I also spent time praying for others.

I remember one time kneeling by the bed with my grandmother as she prayed. She prayed for by name every single one of her family members. She prayed for world leaders and people who were not saved. I fell asleep while my grandmother prayed.

Being a *prayer warrior* and praying for others can be a wonderful, powerful experience.

What better place to go than the feet of Jesus when experiencing fear, conflict, or pain. Who better to talk to about the needs of my friends? However, I have come to realize that I want to spend time with the One who sees me, knows me, and loves me. I need time with the Lover of my soul.

My prayer life over the years has changed. I have learned that to spend precious moments in prayer with God is to experience time with my Friend and Lover of my soul. I don't have to be in conflict or pain to spend time with my Friend, Daddy, and Lover of my soul. Union with God is what I seek in my prayer life.

For me, more of God will not come through *doing* for him but of *being* with him. God desires union with us. It is mind-blowing for me to realize that God wants union with me! God wants conversations with us. God wants our hearts. God desires to be the center of our universe. Is he the center of your universe? How can we make him the center of our universe? I believe that prayer is a good place to start.

Unfortunately, I haven't always been aware of the need to make Jesus the center of my universe. So many times, I have thought only about myself, my hurts, and my needs. I suppose all of us have a tendency to focus on our own *stuff.*

As you know, life is difficult. I am sure that you also know that marriage is hard work.

It just is. Sometimes marriages don't survive the many challenges of life, living life together, and working through our baggage that we bring into the marriage. Sadly, my marriage ended in divorce.

Both my ex-husband and I have survived our divorce with the help of God as well as a program—*divorce recovery workshop*. God has helped both of us in the healing process after divorce.

Going through a divorce is a difficult process, to say the least. It seems logical to me that in the difficult time of divorce, the church family would be there with the ones suffering to offer support and love. What I found instead were people ready to "cast the first stone."

My next story tells about those who cast the first stone.

Kintsugi

I can't believe I am in a divorce recovery workshop. I also can't believe that I am in a singles group at church. It isn't supposed to be this way. I was supposed to be married until "till death us do part." What happened? Were we not meant for each other? Did we stop loving each other? Did we give up too soon? At this point, I suppose there are more questions than answers. Here I am, trying to *recover* from the pain of divorce. What better place to recover than in the safety of a church environment. Or so you would think.

I didn't realize the depth of my hurt until two well-meaning ladies asked to meet with me. They got right to the point and told me that God hates divorce. Divorce is wrong and under no circumstances should I allow a divorce to happen. They were very clear that divorce is a sin—an unforgiveable sin. They also declared that I could not be a witness for Jesus as a divorced woman. "How could you possibly be a role model for others?" they asked.

They did not ask me the questions that I needed them to ask. I suppose it never crossed their minds to ask, How are you? How can we pray for you? How can we pray for your soon-to-be ex-husband? How can we help? What do you need?

The pain of their words stung worse than a bee. The accusations of their words hurt me to the core of my being. If God hates divorce, does he hate me? I know I have done bad things. Is this the ultimate bad sin?

Apparently, the purpose of meeting with me was to hurl accusations. There were no questions, no compassion, and no understanding given that day. What was given instead was "well intended" advice: do not get a divorce. God hates divorce.

A few of us of differing ages met together to form a singles group at church. A young woman who had recently joined the group told me one day that she would no longer be coming to the group. She further said that we could no longer be friends. Shocked, I asked her what had changed. She said that she had a conversation with her parents about our singles group. She told them that a few young people attended the group as well as a couple of divorced people. Her parents advised her not to go back to the group. They also suggested that it was probably not a good idea to be friends with a divorced woman.

They told her that divorced women hate men and marriage. They suggested to her that since I am in the process of getting a divorce, I would not be a healthy influence on her life. They suggested that she stop going to the singles group and stop having a friendship with a divorced woman.

More than feeling hurt by the conversation, I feel sad. It is sad that people think this way. It is sad that they have the mistaken view of God that he would hate the sin so much that he would want others to avoid the "sinner." It is sad that they do not rejoice in knowing that God loves us with all of our spots and blemishes. He loves us in our brokenness.

Dear friend.

According to Japanese legend, the favorite tea cup of shogun Ashikaga Yoshimasa somehow became broken. He sent the tea cup to China to be repaired, and it was returned mended with staples. Displeased with the ugly repairs, he asked a contemporary Japanese craftsman to find a way to repair his treasured tea cup. Thus, *kintsugi* art was born.

In the *kintsugi* art form, broken ceramics are mended with a lacquer resin mixed with powdered gold. The broken places are repaired with the beautiful gold mixture. They are no longer ugly damaged vessels but, rather, beautiful works of art. In fact, Japanese repaired vessels were so popular that artisans would break pottery just so they could be made more beautiful when repaired with gold.

Every single one of us has experienced brokenness. Some of us have experienced the brokenness of divorce. Words spoken over us can result in broken places within our heart as well. Our personal struggles can bring us to a place of brokenness before God.

The beauty of brokenness before God is that he makes something beautiful from our brokenness and pain. *Kintsugi* means "golden joinery" in Japanese. It is in our "golden joinery" with Jesus that we are made beautiful. Only Jesus can take those broken places in our lives and tum them into beauty.

I love it that we do not need to hide our broken places but, instead, embrace our brokenness and allow the healing grace of Jesus to turn the broken places into beauty. We become even more beautiful than we were before our brokenness, so much so that we can praise him for the brokenness that allowed him to make someone beautiful in us.

Being divorced is not something that we need to hide. I know that God can take the pain of divorce and turn our experience and pain into a beautifully restored life, possibly even better than before the divorce. Our *golden joinery* with Jesus is a place of restoration and love. I want you to know that you are a beautiful vase, mended by the gold of God's love.

I would like to share with you one more chapter in my friendship with Georgene.

Fried Green Tomatoes

To my delight, I got a package in the mail from Georgene. I was so excited because she always sends me the best Christmas and birthday presents and, sometimes, a gift for no particular reason at all. I always look forward to Christmas presents from Georgene because they are always unique. One year, she sent me an amazing cross. It is ceramic with a three-dimensional nativity scene on it. One of my favorite gifts is See's candy. I am always excited to receive See's candy. I could hardly wait to see what cool gift Georgene had sent to me.

What in the world! Fried Green Tomatoes! Why would she send this to me? I wondered. It is a wonderful story of love and friendship, but Ruth dies of cancer in the end. That could not be our story. Our story could not end like the movie. Georgene will not die of cancer. She said that the doctor is optimistic that she will recover. I needed to talk to her.

"Georgene, thanks for the movie. Tell me, how are you? Has the doctor run more tests?" I asked.

"Rita, hospice care is coming," declared Georgene.

"Wait, hospice care only comes when someone is dying. What about the treatments? You said that the doctor was optimistic. You can't be dying. You can't die," I cried.

"Rita, keep praying. We are praying. Can you come home? I need you to come."

"Where is the hammer? I can never find the right tool when I need it," I said to myself. Finally, I found the hammer.

"I am going to smash *Fried Green Tomatoes* to bits! This is a horrible story. You should never have to watch someone you love die. Life is not fair. I hate it. I need to beat something. I hate that Georgene is dying. She doesn't deserve to die," I cried.

"Lord, I am a jerk. I'm divorced, not that good of a mom, and not that good of a friend. Why can't you take me instead? Why my precious Georgene?' I cried out to God.

I hate it that people come into my life and, just like that, are too soon gone. Why can't love and friendship and beauty last forever? I hate death. I hate people leaving me. "Jesus, please don't let Georgene die. Please!" I cried.

Dear friend,

I have so many precious memories of time spent with Georgene during high school and college. One of my favorite times shared with Georgene was when we would go to McDonald's for french fries and a Coke. There was no dining inside, so we would sit in the car and talk. Once in a while, a carload of cute boys would show up, and we would stare at them and giggle, trying not to let them know that we were staring.

After I got married and moved to Virginia, I returned to California every summer to visit my family. The trips continued after my girls were born. Georgene had boys the same age as my girls. I suppose my favorite memories with her family are the times that we went camping together on the beach. My girls and Georgene's boys had so much fun together. Even though they only saw each other in the summer, they always picked up right where they left off.

Georgene was the one whom I called when my mother called and told me the horrible news that my brother Johnny Wayne died. Mom told me that there was uncertainty surrounding his death, which made it even more difficult to grasp. He either fell or was pushed from a hotel window while in Hawaii.

I was crying so hard; I could barely speak. Georgene began talking to me without knowing what was wrong, assuring me of God's love for me no matter the situation. Even though she was over two thousand miles away, she was always a phone call away, ready to encourage, laugh with, or to talk to about not much of anything. I am grateful for the amazing shared memories with my dear friend Georgene.

Two months after Georgene went to be with Jesus, I got a phone call from my brother-in-law, telling me that my mom was in the hospital and that the doctors found seven lesions on her brain from melanoma cancer. There was no treatment or cure at this stage. He told me that I needed to come home to California.

My mom was eighty-one years old when she died. We can expect that our parents will die in their eighties or nineties. However, nothing prepares us for their passing. I am grateful that I was with my mom when she died. I got to kiss her goodbye and tell her that I love her.

I am especially grateful that I hold in my heart the memories of my mom in a positive and affirming light. It is with fondness that I recall celebrating her eightieth birthday with her and our family. During that visit, we laughed and shared our fondest memories of our growing-up years. I am so grateful that God allowed me to spend joyful times with my mom in her later years.

I believe that God gives us our family and friends for mutual enjoyment, encouragement, support, godly advice as well as admonishment and accountability. It is so easy in the business of life to take for granted those we love. I suggest that you call, text, or go see those you love as often as you can. As a matter of fact, why not put this book down for now and contact a family member or friend and tell them that you love them. This could be the exact day that someone you love needs to hear from you. Times spent with our family and friends are precious times. They are too quickly gone.

Are you ready to read about an awesome day? I am so ready to tell you a story about ministry shared with my friend Gerry.

What an Awesome Day

G erry and I always meet up at her house to prepare for our day. We gather the goodies for the women's Bible study, visuals for our songs for the kids club, flannel graph pictures, easel as well as candy to give out to the kids.

We go to different places each day to teach kids, single moms, or senior citizens. Each day is different. I would love to share with you the ministry that Gerry and I are so blessed to enjoy. We have an awesome time.

Our first stop is a Bible study with some lovely women at a complex for senior citizens. We so much enjoy meeting with these six or so women. They are so friendly and sweet. One day, Peggy showed up, not to join the Bible study but just to see what was going on.

Peggy had schizophrenia and, most of the time, refused to take her meds. She told us that at one time, she taught at William & Mary. It is difficult to imagine her in the role of a professor since she obviously didn't shower or change clothes. What she did know how to do was to speak in colorful, inappropriate language. She wasn't the favorite resident around the complex. She was the one others chose to avoid.

One day, Peggy came in fussing and fuming. We weren't sure what she was mad about. The other ladies were definitely uncomfortable and didn't want anything to do with her. Gerry and I talked to Peggy and asked how we could help. We never did understand why she was so mad, but it seemed she just wanted to yell, and so we let her. She finally calmed down and relaxed her demeanor. She didn't join the group, but we gained a new friend that day. She would show up sometimes before or after our time with the group and tell us about her life before her illness.

Eventually, Peggy left the complex because she didn't pay her rent. She lived alone in the woods. She would call us once in a while, and we would try to help in the ways that we could. We loved Peggy but were helpless to give her what she needed—medical attention and a place to live. What we did give her was acceptance and love. Eventually, she took a bus to another state to live with a friend. We never heard from her again.

Our next stop is a housing complex in a nearby city. After school, the kids meet us at the complex recreation center. They would come in loud and excited

At the Bible club, we sing songs like "Stop and let me tell you what the Lord has done for me." They are simple songs, but the kids love them. We use attention-getting visuals to show the lyrics. We tell Bible stories and hand out candy as the kids shout out the answers to our review questions. Then we finish with a flannel graph Sunday School Charlie story. In the story, Charlie or someone else always manages to get into trouble. In the end, they do the right thing, and all ends well.

On different days, we go different places. My favorite place to go is the small African American church. They have a church bus, and a church member drives to a nearby neighborhood and loads the bus with active, fully alive kids. They come to the church ready to hear Bible stories, sing songs, get some candy, and hear about the latest adventure of Sunday School Charlie.

I don't know who has more fun, Gerry and me or the kids. We love making connections with the kids and hearing about their lives. Many kids have accepted Jesus into their lives and have started going to that small church on Sundays.

At one location that we go to, we started a softball team that competed in a league of churches. What a challenge to try to "coach" a softball team. We don't know anything about coaching, but we know that the kids love being on a team, learning how to play as well as learning good sportsmanship. I loved their enthusiasm and self-confidence.

In order to play, we needed at least two girls. One girl had never played, but she was certain that she would be the best player to ever pick up a ball. She said that she would be our pitcher. It was more difficult than she thought, but she never gave up. What an inspiration she was to me. We actually won a few games. Maybe Gerry and I knew how to be coaches after all. Ha-ha. What was important was allowing the kids the opportunity to play on a team.

That's it. That is our awesome time, sharing Jesus and his love with others. What blessed days we have had! Partnering with my dear friend Gerry to share the love of Jesus with kids, as well as adults, was one of the greatest blessings of my life.

Dear friend.

Teaching kids is one of the greatest joys of my life. I simply love hanging out with kids and talking to them. I love their energy, honesty, and ability to love without conditions. There are two main reasons that I love sharing Jesus with kids and teaching biblical truths: kids need Jesus as their Savior, and kids need to learn biblical truths that are applicable to their everyday life at school. They need truths that can change their daily lives at school as well as at home.

Another reason that I love sharing Jesus with kids is that they are able to accept and believe biblical truth so easily. Jesus instructed us to come to him like little children.

Children can readily accept that Jesus loves them. They are also keenly aware of sin in their life and can appreciate that Jesus died for their sins. It seems like it is so easy for a child to come to Jesus.

Kids need to know with all their heart that their faith in Jesus as well as their Christlike behavior is relevant to their life at school as well as at home. I love to look for opportunities to share with kids how Jesus and Christlike behavior are relevant every single day in all situations. Let me give a very personal example.

For a couple of summers, I taught at a Christian camp for kids. I taught the day camp.

A bunch of kids being active in the hot sun all day, getting hot, tired, and sometimes grumpy allowed for plenty of opportunities to teach biblical truths—truths like forgiveness, patience, and love.

My grandkids attended for a week each summer. My grandson, Grayson, is very competitive and loved playing a game at camp called GaGa ball. The kids play the game in an enclosed circle and try to kick a ball in such a way that the ball hits the legs of another kid, and then that kid is out. It seems that in this game, arguments are sure to happen. I often heard words like "The ball touched you!" "No, it didn't. I didn't feel it." "You cheated" "You are a liar." Blah, blah, blah.

Grayson would sometimes be in the middle of such arguments. He, as well as the other kids, learned very quickly that they needed to show patience, kindness, and forgiveness to each other as verbal fights erupted. What a perfect teachable moment!

After apologies were said on both sides, the kids would shake hands or hug and go on to the next activity, completely forgiving and forgetting. What would always surprise me was that I would see two boys who, not long ago, were ready to tear each other apart, talking and laughing together.

Even though Grayson is competitive, he wants to play fair and do the right thing. I believe that to be true of kids. They want to live like Christ; they just need to be shown what a Christlike behavior looks like. I was sorta' glad when conflict arose so that we could talk about concepts like patience, kindness, asking for and receiving forgiveness and love.

So often when I am teaching or sharing Jesus with kids, I see in their eyes an eagerness to hear what I am saying. Let me give you an example. Last year, my granddaughter and I went to a mother-daughter weekend. My daughter, Kristy, graciously allowed me to take Zaylee.

My friend Amy led the conference. Amy said that while she was speaking, she noticed that Zaylee sat on the edge of her seat and was taking in every word that Amy was saying. Zaylee was eager to hear the words about Jesus and his love. So often, kids are eager to learn about Jesus.

By the way, I gotta tell you that Zaylee and I took second place in the cupcake wars contest that weekend! Hooray for Grandma and Zaylee! I heard rumors that Amy and her girls should have won, but it would look rigged if the speaker and her girls won. We will never know. Ha-ha-ha.

There are kids who are open and eager to learn. I love those kids. I also love those kids who aren't quite sure what to believe. There are also kids who say they don't care. I know that deep within they do care but have been so wounded they hide who they truly are. My heart goes out to those kids as well. So often, those are the wounded kids who simply need extra love and attention.

There are also unseen kids. They are the ones who often won't follow the rules, get into trouble, or sit quietly in the back of the classroom with their heads down, covered by their hoodie. They are unseen in that they work very hard to hide pain or sadness or who they truly are.

The forgotten kid is the shy one who talks very little, so we, as teachers or leaders, often forget to call on them or talk to them. They become forgotten ones. I have a heart for those kids as well. I see the forgotten and unseen kid. I love them, and I want them to know Jesus and his love.

Come with me as I tell you a story about my night school class of boys. Due to wrong choices, they were suspended from regular classes. On the surface, they look like trouble. I have a heart for the kid who doesn't always do the right thing or make the right decision. I love my night school boys.

The Unseen Kids

In the classroom where we meet for night school, at the back of the classroom on a shelf, there were some unusual animal shapes made from paper. Since we were meeting in a math classroom, the animal shapes were probably a math project that the regular class was working on. One of my night school students decided that it would be fun to play with the cool animal shapes. He and a friend tossed the cool different-shaped animals to each other. When I saw what they were doing, I asked them to give the animals to me and then sit down. It was time for class to begin.

As they were walking back to their seats, our principal walked in. She saw the animals I was holding and asked if we were going to work on a project. I told her that these cool animals belonged to the daytime students. I explained that a couple of boys decided to play around before class started.

She walked over to where the boys were sitting and firmly said, "You need to know that this lady is your best friend right now. Another teacher might have kicked you out of school immediately for this kind of behavior. You do know this is your last chance of getting an education, right?"

They both apologized. She smiled and left the room.

"Are you really my best friend?" one of the boys asked, laughing.

"Yep, if you need a best friend, I'm the one. I could use a best friend," I replied.

He looked surprised and asked why I would want a kid for a best friend.

"Truthfully, sometimes I think that I would rather hang out with you than a lot of adults I know. I think that you have a lot to say, and I want to hear it. Yep, it would be cool to have you guys as friends. I am pretty boring, so you might do better with more fun friends," I laughingly said. "You need to have friends who will encourage you to do well in school and stay out of trouble."

I know that night school kids got into trouble by making poor choices. However, I also know that they are not the mistake that they made or the bad attitude they sometimes show or not even the fake person they want others to see. These kids often try not to let others see, but I do know that they are curious and want to learn, but learning is sometimes difficult for them.

Dear friend,

Probably the most significant encouragement that I have received came when I was in the teacher education program at Christopher Newport College. On a written assignment that I completed, my professor gave it back with a note that encouraged my heart so much. She wrote that someday, I would be a "champion for the forgotten and unseen children." I wasn't completely certain what she meant, but I did know that I often felt like I was an unseen kid and student. No one seemed to see the pain I felt after Tony died.

I was an A student in my early years. Then my best friend and brother died. Nothing seemed to matter after Tony died—not schoolwork, not friends.

As I look back, I believe that in some ways, I was an unseen and forgotten kid. I was quiet and didn't get into trouble at school, and I completed my assignments. The quiet student is sometimes the forgotten student. You know that kid—the one who sits quietly, hoping not to get called on. That kid is often forgotten. I have found that the quiet kid often has a lot of ideas and thoughts worth hearing, if you can only get them to talk. I was unseen in that I did not let anyone see the shame, pain, and worthlessness that I felt. I kept my thoughts hidden.

I sometimes wonder if all of us have that unseen part of who we are.

How many of us are waiting to be seen and heard? It could be that we fear that we would not be loved or accepted if people saw the person that we are on the inside. I also wonder if we have allowed the lies of Satan to keep us from becoming the person who God created us to be. I believe that when we believe the lies from Satan, he steals from us our true identity and purpose—the person who God created us to be.

My aunt Blendena was a teacher in a one-room school in Kansas. I went with her to school a few times. Since it was a one-room school, the kids were all ages. My aunt Blendena loved her kids and told me a little about each kid. I was surprised that she knew so much about each and every kid. She knew their strengths as well as weaknesses.

As a kid, it seemed to me that Granddad and Aunt Blendena knew everything there was to know. I remember thinking that I wanted to be a teacher so that someday I could know about a lot of cool things about other countries and all about science and how things work. Teaching sounded so fun!

Even though I knew in high school that I wanted to be a teacher, I didn't believe that I was smart enough to become a teacher. The words that my mom spoke to me seemed to stick like glue. They wouldn't leave. In my heart, I heard over and over, "I don't know who is dumber, you or John."

I do not believe that she truly felt I was dumb. Maybe she was just having a bad day. It could be that I did something that was "dumb" in that moment. However, at that moment, as a child, I was not capable of thinking it through and realizing that my mom truly did not think that I am dumb. I took her words literally, and the lies were believed as truth.

After Tony died, I lost interest in school. My grades suffered. I convinced myself that I could not learn. I was listening to lies from Satan, even though I did not know it at the time.

It wasn't until I was fifty-one that I received my teaching certificate! Isn't that crazy! I wonder to myself sometimes if I would have been a teacher at twenty-two if I had not listened to the lies of Satan and believed the words that were spoken over me. Then I realized that kind thinking is of no value to me today.

God has blessed me so much in the opportunities that he has given me to teach the "unseen or forgotten" kids. For a time, I had the pleasure of teaching kids who were suspended from school. I had the great joy of teaching kids as a homebound teacher as well.

Perhaps lies had been spoken over some of these kids as well. It is always my desire to see the strengths in the kids I teach and encourage them to be the people that God created them to be.

I am wondering as I write, what lies were spoken over your life? Were you told that you will never amount to anything? Were you told that you are not good enough? Whatever words of discourage-

THE CENTER OF THE UNIVERSE

ment were spoken over you, God can change those words to words of truth.

We have such an amazing God. He blesses us every single day of our lives. Sometimes we don't pay attention, so we miss his blessings.

Sometimes the pain and hurt of life smacks us in the face, and we forget that God is in every situation in our lives.

Just like my night school boys, we need friends in our lives who will encourage us, love us, and speak truth into our lives to remind us that we can become the women that God created us to be.

By the way, I gotta tell you that my best friend really is a kid, Alora. I told you a little about her in the beginning of our story time together. Actually, she isn't really a kid; she is a teenager. I consider her my best friend, even though she has best friends her own age. I love talking with Alora. She encourages me so much. I love her stories. I love hearing about her hopes and dreams for the future. She has plans of writing a book. I can hardly wait to read it. I love it that Alora has a heart for the forgotten, unseen kids in her school. Alora is amazing!

I love hanging out with kids. You would too, if you took the opportunity. Try talking to a kid about what they want to talk about. You will be glad that you did. Please, please, please don't let a kid that you know go unseen or unheard.

My next story reminds me of God's faithfulness and love. I would love for you to meet my two daughters, Kristy and Lori.

God Is Faithful

Oh, the stories we mommas could tell about our children! We know fun stories, boring stories, exciting stories, sad stories, and even embarrassing stories. I, too, have stories to share about my daughters. What I would love to share with you are stories of God's faithfulness and love in their lives.

Of course, my fistborn, Kristy, was the most beautiful child that God ever created. It is probably true that all moms and dads look at their babies and see in them the most beautiful people ever created! Kristy had big beautiful eyes and a smile that could melt your heart.

Kristy spent the first few months of her life throwing up formula, so she was underweight. Her little body was so tiny, and her eyes were so big that she sorta' reminded me of a little bird! Now you are probably thinking, *What a horrible thing to say about your baby!* I know. I'm sorry! She just was not the chubby baby she was supposed to be, and I certainly didn't know what to do about it. The doctor said that nothing was wrong with her. To make matters even worse, I was told that I should not breastfeed due to thyroid issues. I now know that was not correct.

When I took Kristy to California to see my family, my mom asked me what was wrong with the doctors. I told her that they were no help in figuring out why she couldn't keep formula down. Anyway, with much trial and error and a lot help from my mother, we found a formula that she could keep in her tummy. Soon thereafter, she became a normal chubby baby.

The US Army sent us to Germany when Kristy was a toddler. My beautiful German neighbor showed me how to braid Kristy's hair and dress her so that she looked like a typical German toddler. I loved it when people in our little village would tell me what a beautiful little girl she was.

As a young woman, Kristy was experiencing abdominal pain, so she went to the doctor. After tests were completed, the doctor told her that he saw a suspicious mass. With further testing, it was revealed that she had a dermoid tumor, which contained teeth and hair. The tumor could have landed anywhere on her body. It attached itself to an ovary.

When she told me about the tumor, I told her that we needed to go immediately to see Pastor Dave so that he could pray for her. When we arrived at his office, he placed his hand on her body and asked God to heal Kristy's body and remove the mass. He also told her that she needed to continue to see her doctor and follow his recommendations.

The doctor scheduled surgery soon after identifying the tumor. After cutting her open, the doctor told Kristy that he could not find the tumor. He said that he had no explanation as to what happened. He told her that God must be on her side and that she was blessed. He then said that the bigger blessing was that he found endometriosis, which had wrapped itself around vital organs. He further said that if he had not found out about the presence of endometriosis, she could have lost her life. She began treatment for the endometriosis. Praise Jesus.

A few years later, Kristy had another medical issue that needed the faithful, miraculous touch of Jesus. I received a frantic phone call from her. She called me from a pay phone crying. She said that she had just left the doctor's office, and he told her that she had ovarian cancer.

"Call Pastor Dave," she cried. "God will heal my cancer. Please call Pastor Dave now."

I called Pastor Dave, and he prayed with me over the phone. Again, God was faithful to hear and answer our prayers. Kristy was healed!

I have one more amazing story in Kristy's life to share with you. When Kristy was a teenager, she sometimes fainted. When I would take her to doctors, they could never come up for a reason for her to faint. One doctor suggested that she would "grow out of it."

A few years later, after she was married, we found out why she was fainting. One day, while in the shower and about to wash her hair, she realized that she could not lift her arms above her head. She called for her then husband, Dennis. She told him that she might be having a heart attack. They agreed that she needed to go to the emergency room.

However, Kristy, like any other *normal* woman, knew that she couldn't go to the emergency room with unwashed hair. Since she couldn't raise her arms, she told Dennis that he had to wash her hair. So into the shower he went and washed her hair before they headed to the emergency room.

At the emergency room, she was immediately hooked up to a heart monitor. The nurse was having difficulty finding a vein to get Kristy hooked up to an IV. With all the poking going on, Kristy was feeling pain. She told the nurse the poking was hurting her, and then she fainted. Not only did she faint, but her heart stopped beating as well.

Dennis began yelling, telling Kristy to wake up. He was hitting her, trying to get her heart to start beating again. He fell on top of her, begging her to wake up.

Quickly, nurses came in and ushered Dennis out of the room as he continued to scream. After several minutes, the nurses were able to get Kristy's heart beating again. Praise Jesus!

When Kristy was conscious and able to talk about what had just happened, she said that she had just had the most amazing dream. She said that she felt so much love and peace, more love than she had ever felt in her life. She was so happy. She saw people in the distance who were very happy to see her. They were happily talking to her. She then heard someone calling her name. She told the people, who she could barely see, that she was sorry that she could not stay. She told them that she had to leave because someone was calling her name. Then she was awake.

Kristy's heart had stopped beating for several minutes. I am not a doctor, so I cannot explain in medical terms what happened. After spending many days in the ICU and many tests later, her cardiologist explained that her heart would stop beating when she was experiencing immense pain. The doctor said that to remedy the situation, she would need a pacemaker. After much discussion, arguing, and convincing, Kristy did get a pacemaker placed in her chest. I think what really convinced her to get it was when the doctor told her that he could take away her driver's license if she did not get a pacemaker.

I am so grateful for Jesus and his faithfulness. I am grateful to Dennis for taking her to the emergency room and yelling her name when her heart stopped beating. I am grateful for the nurses who kept her alive. I am grateful for the cardiologist who was able to successfully diagnose the situation and come up with a solution to keep Kristy's heart from stopping again.

Unfortunately, Dennis and Kristy divorced. However, they remain friends today. Kristy married an awesome man, Eric. They have a beautiful blended family.

I told you stories about Grayson and Zaylee and how awesome they are. Kristy's husband, Eric, lost his wife to a heart attack when Zaylee was just six weeks old. I gotta tell you about how Eric and Kristy met. It reminds me of one of those corny romantic comedies that I love so much.

Grayson and Zaylee were on the same soccer team. At one of the games, Kristy noticed a really handsome dad who came to the games. One day, she noticed him sitting alone in his lawn chair, watching his daughter, Zaylee, play. So Kristy, being the outgoing girl she is, put her lawn chair down right next to this good-looking guy and struck up a conversation. Along came the handsome man's dad. He put his lawn chair down between Kristy and the handsome dad. Kristy struck up a conversation with him as well, long-lost friends enjoying a soccer game together!

Kristy's friend saw an opportunity to be a matchmaker. She gave the good-looking guy, Eric, a team schedule. On the schedule, she wrote Kristy's phone number. How cool is that? Well, he called Kristy soon after and asked her to go on a date with him. She said yes, and now they are happily married. Eric is a wonderful, thoughtful, caring guy. They have a beautiful blended family. Isn't that a great story?

Kristy would never refer to Zaylee as her stepdaughter. Zaylee is her daughter in every way. It is so awesome that Grayson and Zaylee became instant friends as well as siblings. Zaylee watches out for her brother, and he is lost without her. Kristy calls them her "blended twins." If you ask Zaylee about her brother, she will tell you that he is her blended twin. Don't you just love it?

What I would like for you to know about Kristy is that she has a generous heart. When she hears about a need of a friend or stranger, she will get on the phone to find help or use her personal finances to meet that need. She has a heart for helping and loving others.

My other daughter, Lori, has a heart of service. She has volunteered for Habitat for Humanity as well as served with a group from our church on a mission trip to Honduras. I was blessed to be able to go on the mission trip with Lori and her son, Johnathan. Let me tell you a little bit about that trip.

Honduras is very hot in the summer. Lori does not do well with heat. She often suffers from heat exhaustion. Every summer that we went to Disneyland, she would throw up due to the heat. Her body simply cannot tolerate heat. She was determined not to let the heat keep her from having fun at Disneyland or anything else that she wants to do.

For a couple of days while we were in Honduras, Lori went door-to-door with other team members, praying for the villagers and sharing the love of Jesus with them. Her face was beet red, and she was exhausted, but she did not stop going door-to-door. Amazingly, she did not throw up. She was determined to share her faith with others, even if she got hot and threw up. However, God protected her. Not one time did she throw up. She was determined to go into the village and share the love of Jesus with others. I praise Jesus for her heart's desire to share the love of Jesus with others, even when she was hot and exhausted.

Johnathan helped the leader who told Bible stories to the kids of the village. He played games with them, laughed with them, and shared his heart of love with them. He was taking Spanish in school so was able to talk to the kids a little. His Spanish-speaking ability came in handy when we went to the mall and ordered food at a restaurant.

Johnathan does not do well in social situations. Yet he seemed at ease hanging out with the kids in Honduras. I praise Jesus that Johnathan loved the village kids and was willing to come out of his comfort zone to share himself and Jesus with them.

The one thing that I want you to know about my girls is that they both have a heart and a love to serve others. For that, I am grateful. I am grateful for God's faithfulness in blessing the lives of my daughters.

Dear friend,

Lest you think that we are a perfect family, let me just tell you right now that we are not. My husband and I divorced. Our family has unresolved issues that need to be dealt with, just like many other families. It is so easy to look at another person, couple, or family and feel jealousy or envy. We do not walk their daily path with them, so we do not see what struggles and burdens they carry every day.

It shouldn't, but it always surprises me when I hear about the struggles of families who, on the surface, look like they have the perfect marriage and perfect "straight A" kids. There are no perfect marriages, perfect families, or perfect people. We only find those "perfect families" in beautifully staged family photos posted on Facebook. I bet the "perfect" family is hanging on your wall right now.

My favorite photos are the ones where that one kid does his own thing. My favorite photo of Grayson is with his school classmates. Everyone has nice smiles and cute clothes. Then there is Grayson with both hands in the air with a touchdown stance. So great!

Family life, marriages, and true friendships are often messy and sometimes difficult.

Our enemy, Satan, knows how to *get to us*. He knows how to use our weaknesses against us to try to destroy our families. The enemy throws so much at us to try to make us feel isolated, abandoned, and alone—even within families.

One thing that we can know for certain is that God is faithful. He is faithful to be with us in the unbearable times of suffering and pain as well as the times of great joy and rejoicing. I have seen so many times God's handiwork and faithfulness in the life of my children.

Another thing that I know for certain is that God is at work in your life as well as the life of your family. I pray for you that God will strengthen your family. Your family is not perfect, but they are your family. Let your family know that you love them. I pray God's blessings on your family. I also ask you to pray for my family as well. Are you ready to hear my falling in love with Jesus story? I am ready to share that experience with you.

Falling in Love

I love listening to the worship team practice before the worship service. I serve in KidPoint, so I am often teaching kids during the worship service. One Sunday, after I set up my teaching environment at KidPoint, I went into the worship center for my time of worship and praise. As the band began playing the song "Forever Reign," I saw the words on the screen and sang them from a place deep in my heart. "You are good / you are good when there's nothing good in me / You are love / you are love on display for all to see." My heart seemed to open as I sang this *love song* to Jesus.

As I continued to sing, I was fully and completely singing to Jesus with all that was within me, "I'm running to your arms / I'm running to your arms," I sang. I was no longer on my feet. I fell on my knees, and for the first time in my life, I was kneeling before my wonderful Savior and Lover of my soul, crying—crying tears of relief, joy, and love. My experience of praise, love, and worship was like none other in my entire life. After the song, I praised Jesus in prayer and then returned to the KidPoint area a different person, filled with peace and joy!

I decided to share my experience with Pastor Eric and his wife, my friend Amy.

As I was talking to them, our friend David showed up. I told David about my worship experience. He smiled broadly and told me that it sounded like I fell in love with Jesus in that precious moment. He told me that he, too, experienced a special time of falling in love with Jesus. He agreed; falling in love with Jesus is unlike any other experience. It is life-changing.

Yes! That it is. I fell in love with Jesus. The presence of Jesus was so real and powerful that day. My soul erupted in love for the one who "loves me when there is nothing good in me." My heart was awakened as I sang, "God is love, on display for me to see." My heart and soul's response was falling in love with Jesus. We love Jesus, but to *fall in love with Jesus* takes our relationship to an all new level.

Dear friend,

Isn't it exciting and fun to *fall in love*. Have you ever been around someone who recently fell in love? Everything is beautiful to them. The person in love sees everything through the eyes of love. They could have a flat tire, spilled coffee, or any myriad of bad stuff happen but not be fazed in the slightest. All is right with the world because they are *in love*.

When you are truly in love with Jesus, life might just look a little different to you. Not that you will be worry free and happy all the time. However, when hard times come, you will know who is with you. In your deepest sorrow, pain, or disappointment, Jesus is as close as your breath. In the midst of whatever happens in your life, you can know joy—true joy.

Do you remember me telling you about my friend Amy? She is the one who encouraged me to share my story with you. I cannot share her personal love story with Jesus, but I can share what I saw one dark day.

Amy and her wonderful husband Josh lost a child. While in the hospital, surrounded by family and friends, Amy asked for her cell phone. She turned on a song of victory and praise, "See a Victory." She was able to praise the lover of her soul. Only the true lover of her soul could comfort her. Since Amy is deeply in love with Jesus, she knew victory in this dark hour could only come from turning to Jesus, the true Comforter, Strength, and Lover of her soul.

My relationship with Jesus is a journey. My relationship began when, as a teenager, I invited Jesus into my life. Many sermons, conferences, experiences as well as godly relationships have pointed me to Jesus and his love.

My relationship with Jesus is very real and personal. He is the true Lover of my soul.

Others accept the love of Jesus easier than I have. My friend Pastor Penny told me that her Sunday school teacher told her that Jesus loves her. She was able to accept that love and freely gives her life and love for Jesus. Penny fell in love with Jesus as a child. As an adult, she shares the love of Jesus with others as a pastor as well as a friend to many people.

Over the years, Pastor Penny has patiently and faithfully guided me to a deeper relationship with Jesus. She has helped me to realize that all through my life and experiences, Jesus has been there with me, loving me through every single situation. His love has never failed me.

My prayer for you is that you will meet Jesus in a personal way, fall in love and know Jesus in a very personal way.

The final chapter of my story takes us back to Coffeyville, Kansas, to the home of my aunt Blendena and uncle Bernard. It is a time of joy and innocence.

Kay Baby

I love coming to see Aunt Blendena and Uncle Bernard. I just cross the street, cut between houses, and here I am at Aunt Blendena's house. Aunt Blendena loves it when I come to visit. I can tell that she loves me. She always smiles and says, "Hi, Rita Kay."

I love seeing my cousins, Yvonne and Jimmy. Yvonne sure does like to give kisses.

Every time she sees me, she gives me so many kisses. I pretend like I don't like it, but I love her kisses. My other cousin, Jimmy, is so awesome. He has such cool stuff in his room. He has a machine that he can use to show cartoons on the wall. Isn't that cool! He also has books and magic stuff. He has so much magic stuff. He is probably a real magician. I don't know where he gets all his cool stuff.

My granddad is here too. Sometimes he comes to my house to see me and Tony, but he lives here with Aunt Blendena and Uncle Bernard. I wish that he lived with me.

Uncle Bernard always picks me up when he sees me. And then he laughs. I don't know why. He just laughs when I come over to see him. Uncle Bernard is funny and great.

When Aunt Blendena saw me walk into the kitchen, she said, "Hi, Rita Kay. What do you want for breakfast? I have eggs."

"No," I told her. "I want toast and hot cocoa."

I love how Aunt Blendena cuts the toast, not straight across but sideways. I can dunk the pointy end of the toast in my hot cocoa. Aunt Blendena always has hot cocoa on the stove.

Uncle Bernard walked in and said, "Kay Baby, hi! I am glad you are here to have breakfast with us."

Uncle Bernard gave me the biggest hug. I love it when Uncle Bernard calls me Kay Baby. I know that I am not a baby, but he always smiles so big when he says it, so I know it is good to be Kay Baby.

Yvonne came in the room and smiled when she saw me. I got my usual kisses from my cousin Yvonne.

"Where is Jimmy?" I asked. "He is gonna be late for breakfast."

Then Jimmy walked in. He didn't say anything. I don't think he likes getting up in the morning. I love Jimmy so much.

After breakfast, Granddad lit up one of his Camel cigarettes.

"Make smoke circles," I begged Granddad. "I love your smoke circles."

As he blew the smoke from the cigarette into smoke circles, I laughed with delight. Only Granddad blows smoke into circles. Aunt Blendena smokes Camel cigarettes too, but she can't make circles of smoke like Granddad.

Granddad asked me if I wanted to walk with him to the store.

"We don't have any candy in this house. I think that we need to walk across the street and see if we can find some candy."

"Yes!" I yelled. "Let's go to the store to get candy."

Dear friend,

We have made a complete circle, and here we are, back in Coffeyville, Kansas. For the first six years or so of my life, my family and I lived in Coffeyville Kansas, just a short block away from my dad's sister and her husband, two cousins, and my granddad.

Tony and I spent a lot of time at Aunt Blendena's house. Johnny Wayne was just a baby, so he didn't go to Aunt Blendena's house often.

What great times were spent in Coffeyville! We sometimes played Monopoly or cards. In the summer months, we took turns turning the crank on the wooden ice-cream maker. When it got too difficult to turn, we knew the ice cream was ready. Aunt Blendena would then scoop the ice cream into metal cups for us to eat.

When it got dark, the neighbors, Uncle Bernard, Aunt Blendena, and Granddad could be found sitting outside in the backyard on their metal lawn chairs, smoking and talking. We kids would play kick-the-can or hide-and-seek. Sometimes, we got canning jars from the kitchen and would catch fireflies and put them in our jars. What fun we had!

So often, my heart goes back to that time. It was a time of innocence. It was a time before meeting that sick kid, a time before Tony died as well as a time of experiencing deep joy and love. I sometimes yearn to go back to that time of innocence, joy, and love.

Sometimes I think in my heart that it would be wonderful if I could get on a plane, fly to Kansas, walk into the house on 13 East Martin Street and hear, "Hi, Rita Kay Baby! We have missed you. We love you. Welcome home. Let's eat breakfast and then go to the store to get candy."

I want to tell you what is even more wonderful. After I take my final breath, I will be greeted with "Rita Kay Baby! You are home. I love you! Come with me to the banquet table. You never have to leave. We will be together forever." I will be completely engulfed in the love of my Father and his Son, Jesus.

That is it, my dear friend; the true desire at the depth of our heart is complete union with God. Our hunger and desire for love and wholeness can only be satiated in the presence of pure love—in the presence of God. Like the song says, I can only imagine how my heart will feel.

Do you remember the iced tea commercial where the guy falls backward into the pool? I wonder if that is what it will be like for me, falling into his love so as to be completely immersed and surrounded by pure love and joy. It blows my mind to try to comprehend heaven.

You know what else blows my mind? God promises me that I can live life to the fullest right now today. My hope is in heaven, but I am living out my life today. My life today can be spent living life to the fullest, seeking union with God, meeting him in worship and praise as well as quiet moments in my heart, making him the center of my universe. This verse says it all for me:

I am the gate; whoever enters through me will be saved. They come in and go out and find pasture. The thief comes only to steal and kill and destroy; I have come that they may have life, and have it to the full. (John 10:910)

That is it, my friend, the great story that we can experience every single day: living life to the fullest, right now, today, with our Lord Jesus Christ. I pray that you will be reminded daily who you are in Christ and live your life and your story to the fullest.

Please pray for me that I, too, will remember who I am and that I will strive to live each day to the fullest and walk in the truth that I am loved.

GEMS

My friend Emily often sends me encouraging texts. So often in the text, she will say to me, "You are a gem." That word of encouragement always makes me smile. What I have come to realize is that in creating women, God created gems—precious, beautiful, sparkling gems. In addition to creating beautiful gems, he created in women the ability to encourage, strengthen, and impart wisdom to each other.

So often, we don't see the true beauty that God created in us. We see our mistakes, brokenness, and failures. Our true beauty is easier seen by other women than ourselves. As we come together to share our stories, we learn to see ourselves as God sees us—the gems he created us to be.

Each of us has a story just waiting to be told. In our shared stories, the time, place, and events are different. However, the need for the healing touch of Jesus is the same. In our shared stories, we realize that we are not alone. We see the One who unites us, the One who is the true center of our universe. Through sharing our story with other women, we receive much-needed encouragement, strength, and wisdom.

Your story, as well as your wisdom, strength, and encouragement, is needed in the lives of other women. You might be thinking that you are not wise, strong, or an encourager. I get it. Most days I do not feel wise, strong, or capable of encouraging others either. However, when we step back and look at our lives, we will see the truth, light, and love of Jesus in our story. He has been there with us all along. When we stop believing the lies of the enemy and step into being the women that God created us to be, then we can offer his wisdom, strength, and encouragement to others.

If you are like me, it could be that you can say to another woman, "Please don't do what I did. Please make better choices." It is often in our mistakes that we find wisdom.

Your story matters and needs to be heard. You are a precious beautiful gem, and you need to give to others the wisdom, strength, and encouragement that is so desperately needed. As you share your story, you will find that God empowers your story, and you become an encourager for other women.

I encourage you to invite a group of women to meet with you to share your stories. At the end of this book, you will find discussion questions to help guide your GEMS group in sharing your personal stories.

Your GEMS group will strengthen, encourage, and impart wisdom to each other. In your GEMS group, you will see the truth that God Empowers My Story. I would love to hear your story, comments or prayer requests. Feel free to contact me at: ritakayr@gmail.com.

The Center of the Universe

Where Your Story and My Story Meet

Introduction Letter/The Train Station

It is so fun and encouraging to hear how someone triumphed over adversity and came out the victor. You might not have given it much thought, but you, too, have seen victories in your life.

- Tell a time when God gave you the victory in a difficult situation.
- Were there certain things that your mom or dad would say like, "Stop crying, or I will give you something to cry about."
- Did your parents have real eyeball-to eyeball conversations with you when you were young?
- What is your "what if" or "if only" thought from your childhood?
- Have you given up your "what if" or "if only?"
- Did you ever think about wanting a rescuer as a child or teen?
- Describe your rescuer. Was he a prince or maybe a guy on a white horse? Maybe a guy on a motorcycle?
- In a practical way, how can Jesus be our rescuer?

Uncle Paul/Quarantined

God loves us so much that He created the beauty of the Earth for our pleasure.

- Which do you enjoy more, mountains or the beach? Share why. What is your favorite memory being at the beach or the mountains?
- How does God express love to you in a personal way through what He has given you?
- When did you experience hearing Bible stories? Were they real to you or just stories?
- Shame is an unpleasant self-conscious emotion typically associated with a negative evaluation of the self. When you feel shame, you feel like a bad person. Satan wants us to live in shame, believing a lie about who we truly are in Christ.
- Have you had an experience in your life that resulted in feelings of shame?
- Shame is a false identity. Who does Jesus say we are in him?
- How do we step into our true identity in Christ?
- Tell us some good qualities about yourself. What are ways that God has gifted you?

California/Life and Death

- What are your most fun memories as a kid?
- What were the best years of your life?
- Tell us about your siblings. Did you fight or play well together?
- What was your favorite TV show growing up?
- What were your family traditions?
- Tell us about a big *whoosh* in your life? Did you feel physically ill?
- Was anyone with you to help you through the big whoosh?

- Is that big whoosh still causing you pain? Do you need to forgive someone in your whoosh story? Can you forgive them?
- How can Jesus provide healing from your whoosh story?
- If you have found peace, how did that happen?

Jesus

Each of us will come to a place in our lives in which we realize that we need Jesus, not just a get-out-of-hell free card but our Savior and Lover of our soul. It is important to share with others the relationship that we have found in Jesus. We need to share the Good News of who Jesus is in our lives.

- Share when you asked Jesus to come into your life.
- How has your relationship with Jesus changed and grown over the years?
- Was there a time in your life that you strayed from your relationship with Jesus?
- What did you do to *restore* your relationship?
- What are some things that you do to nurture your relationship?

High School/Youth for Christ

High school can be difficult years as we search for our identity. Those years can be embarrassing, tragic, or filled with fun and adventure.

- What are your best high school memories?
- Do you recall a funny or embarrassing moment?
- Who was your favorite teacher? Why?
- Was there a teacher who pushed you or was strict? As an adult, do you appreciate that "push"?
- What was it about your appearance that you struggle with the most?
- What was your biggest high school struggle?

There are times when we know and tell God exactly what we want. We pray, and God does not give us the answer we expect. We sometimes simply need to trust the wisdom of God.

- Has there been a time that you prayed for something, and your prayer was not answered?
- Did that cause you to doubt God or his love?
- Has there been a time that you prayed for something, and God gave you something even better?
- Is there a time that you went forward with your plan without seeking God first?
- Is there a time that you asked for God's guidance, and you saw him work in a particular situation?
- Do you ever ask God to direct your path every day?
- Suppose you have a bad day, and everything goes wrong. Can you step back, maybe laugh and rejoice in God in the midst of a terrible, horrible, very bad day? How do we do that?

Whoosh

Parents, teachers, or sometimes friends say wounding words to us. It may not be intentional, but words matter and can be very wounding. Often words spoken to us can take on a power over our lives and future decisions.

- What were the hurtful false words spoken over you?
- How did those words impact your decisions and actions?
- What is your "go to" negative phrase about yourself that you say?
- What lies would Satan have you believe about yourself?
- Has someone spoken truth over you? Is it difficult to accept and believe?

Have you allowed the truth of who God created you to be sink deep into your soul? Sometimes the lie is easier to believe than the truth. You need to verbally speak the truth of who you are in Jesus.

- What strengths has he given to you? What spiritual gifts has he given to you?
- Look at the 'things to do" section in the book. Are you doing any of those things regularly?
- Speak truth to each other. Look at a member of your group and tell her who you see. Tell her the strengths that you see.

How the West Was Won/Voices

We Christians have a "language" that we speak to each other.

Has it happened that someone spoke words to you that seemed shallow or insincere? Have you ever said that you will pray for someone, then forget to pray?

- What are some common phrases that we say to each other?
- What we are saying is true; however, could it be that the person needs something else? What could they need?
- What voices did you hear when you were younger?
- What did they say to you?
- As a little girl, what dreams did you have for yourself?
- Do you believe that happiness is found in being a wife or a mom?
- Do you take joy in being a wife or a mom?
- Do you find joy in your relationship with Jesus?
- Has there been a time that your kids surprised you with their words of wisdom? Share those times and words.

Is This Love/Together yet Always Apart

Falling in love is a wonderful, powerful experience. Staying in love is a choice.

- Do you remember your first kiss? Was it awkward or magical?
- Who was your first love?
- What did you learn about love with your first love?
- Were there wounded places in your heart that impacted your love relationships?
- Do you agree that love is a choice that we make?
- Have you ever placed a wall around your heart?
- Did someone help you tear down that wall?
- Maybe there are still places in your heart walled up?
- How can we safely remove walls?

The Center of the Universe/Kintsugi

God desires to be the center of our daily lives.
- Have you ever met anyone who seemed to place Jesus as the center of their universe? Tell us about that person.
- What practical things can we do to make Jesus the center of our lives?
- When you first were married, was your spouse the center of your universe?
- Did getting a divorce cost you other friendships?
- Have you healed from your divorce?
- How did you heal from your divorce?
- What did you learn about yourself from your divorce experience?

Fried Green Tomatoes/What an Awesome Day

Who was or is your closest friend? Tell us about that friend.

- What fun things have you done with your closest friends?
- Have you told your friends how important they are to you?
- What are ways that we share our love for each other as friends?
- What are the ways that you express yourself—letters, texts, phone calls, lunch dates?
- What can we do to nurture our relationships?
- What is your passion? What about it gives you great joy?
- Share a recent work or fun experience in which you found great joy.
- Are you living your passion or simply going through the motions?
- What changes can you make in your life to more engage in your passion?

The Unseen Kids/God Is Faithful

Teaching is my passion.

- Do you know any kids who are not seen by others?
- Do you know any kids who are misunderstood by others?
- What can you do to make sure that you give your kids opportunities to be seen and heard?
- Were you seen and heard as a kid?
- Do you feel seen and heard now?

It is so easy to look at other families and feel jealous or wish our family could be like them. If you got to know them, perhaps you would feel differently about your own family dynamics.

What family have you admired from a far?

- Do you have a favorite family photo? If so, what did it take to get that perfect photo?
- Tell about a time that you were proud of your children. What did they do or say?
- Share a funny or embarrassing story about one of your children or a sibling.
- Tell about a time that you struggled and wondered if they would make it to adulthood.
- Tell about a time that you have felt proud of your adult child.

Falling in Love/Kay Baby

- Share your experience of "falling in love" with Jesus.
- Share a special moment when you felt close to God.
- Tell us about your prayer to God. Is he your father, rescuer, friend?

There might be special family member that we love to go see. They have a way of showing us that we are special. It might be a friend and not a family member. There is that someone that we love to visit.

As a kid, did you have a favorite relative that you loved to go see because they were excited to see you?

- Do you have that same experience going to see a relative or friend as an adult?
- What do you do to demonstrate your love and appreciation for kids or adults that come to visit you?
- What can we do to show others that we value them?
- Where is it that you consider home other than the place where you live?
- Have you ever thought what it will be like when we go "home" to Jesus?

- Jesus is preparing a place for you right now. If you could design your home in heaven? What would it look like?
- What can we do now to experience "heaven on earth"?
- Who is the first person that you hope to see in heaven?

About the Author

Rita Kay Reese is a retired teacher. It was her joy to teach and encourage students for over twenty years. She is blessed to have two adult daughters and three grandchildren. Rita currently works at the center of the university Chick-fil-A in Ashland, Virginia, where it is her pleasure to serve great food in a caring atmosphere alongside a great team.

CPSIA information can be obtained
at www.ICGtesting.com
Printed in the USA
BVHW081920160921
616898BV00001B/56